MACMILLAN MODERN DRAMATISTS

Macmillan Modern Dramatists
Series Editors: *Bruce King* and *Adele King*

Published titles

Reed Anderson, *Federico Garcia Lorca*
Eugene Benson, *J. M. Synge*
Renate Benson, *German Expressionist Drama*
Normand Berlin, *Eugene O'Neill*
Michael Billington, *Alan Ayckbourn*
John Bull, *New British Political Dramatists*
Denis Calandra, *New German Dramatists*
Neil Carson, *Arthur Miller*
Maurice Charney, *Joe Orton*
Ruby Cohn, *New American Dramatists, 1960–1980*
Bernard F. Dukore, *American Dramatists, 1918–1945*
Bernard F. Dukore, *Harold Pinter*
Arthur Ganz, *George Bernard Shaw*
James Gibbs, *Wole Soyinka*
Frances Gray, *John Arden*
Julian Hilton, *Georg Büchner*
David Hirst, *Edward Bond*
Helene Keyssar, *Feminist Theatre*
Bettina L. Knapp, *French Theatre 1918–1939*
Charles Lyons, *Samuel Beckett*
Susan Bassnett-McGuire, *Luigi Pirandello*
Jon McDonald, *The New Drama 1900–1914*
Margery Morgan, *August Strindberg*
Leonard C. Pronko, *Eugène Labiche and Georges Feydeau*
Jeanette L. Savona, *Jean Genet*
Claude Schumacher, *Alfred Jarry and Guillaume Apollinaire*
Laurence Senelick, *Anton Chekhov*
Theodore Shank, *American Alternative Theatre*
James Simmons, *Sean O'Casey*
David Thomas, *Henrik Ibsen*
Dennis Walder, *Athol Fugard*
Thomas Whitaker, *Tom Stoppard*
Nick Worrall, *Nikolai Gogol and Ivan Turgenev*
Katharine Worth, *Oscar Wilde*

Further titles are in preparation

MACMILLAN MODERN DRAMATISTS

FRENCH THEATRE
1918—1939

Bettina L. Knapp

Professor of Romance Languages and
Comparative Literature at
Hunter College,
and the Graduate Center,
City University of New York

MACMILLAN

First published 1985

Published by
Higher and Further Education Division
MACMILLAN PUBLISHERS LTD
Houndmills, Basingstoke, Hampshire RG21 2XS
and London
Companies and representatives
throughout the world

Printed in Great Britain by
Typeset by
Wessex Typesetters Ltd, Frome, Somerset

British Library Cataloguing in Publication Data
Knapp, Bettina L.
    French theatre, 1918–1939.—(Macmillan modern
    dramatists)
    1. French drama—20th century—History and criticism
    I. Title
    842'.91209   PQ556

    ISBN 0–333–37258–1
    ISBN 0–333–37259–X Pbk

Contents

Contents

List of Plates

List of Plates

12. Georges Pitoëff in *Le Voyageur sans bagage*, Théâtre des Mathurins, February 1937
13. *Le Voyageur sans bagage*, 1937
14. *Le Partage de Midi*, Théâtre Marigny, 1948, Jean-Louis Barrault, Pierre Brasseur, Edwige Feuillere, Jaques Dacqmine

Editors' Preface

The *Macmillan Modern Dramatists* is an international series of introductions to major and significant nineteenth and twentieth century dramatists, movements and new forms of drama in Europe, Great Britain, America and new nations such as Nigeria and Trinidad. Besides new studies of great and influential dramatists of the past, the series includes volumes on contemporary authors, recent trends in the theatre and on many dramatists, such as writers of farce, who have created theatre 'classics' while being neglected by literary criticism. The volumes in the series devoted to individual dramatists include a biography, a survey of the plays, and detailed analysis of the most significant plays, along with discussion, where relevant, of the political, social, historical and theatrical context. The authors of the volumes, who are involved with theatre as playwrights, directors, actors, teachers and critics, are concerned with the plays as theatre and discuss such matters as performance, character interpretation and staging, along with themes and contexts.

BRUCE KING
ADELE KING

Introduction

11 November 1918. The Armistice. The end of World War I. A spirit of intense joy swept over France. Jazz bands howled out their brash sounds and rhythmic beats; dancing became popular once again; parades filled the streets. Theatre flourished. Entertainment and excitement were the rule of the day. A counterpoise, certainly, to the harsh facts of war: one and a half million Frenchmen had died; countless had suffered in the trenches; still more had been permanently disabled, deprived of a normal future.

After the Armistice, Paris remained a composite of opposites. Its theatres seemed to satisfy the requirements of all classes, all types, all tastes. The classical and historical repertoire of the state subsidised Comédie-Française and Odéon offered the works of France's greats: Corneille, Molière, Marivaux, Musset, Beaumarchais, and so many others. Here young and old alike listened in rapt silence to the declamation of 'sacred' stanzas and monologues they had committed to memory in school.

Other people went to the theatre simply to be enter-

1

tained and distracted. For these individuals, the so-called boulevard theatre answered their needs. Sacha Guitry (1885–1957) was perhaps the most popular dramatist actor of his day. In his stage works, which number one hundred and thirty, we find levity mingling with acrimony, flippancy with seriousness, love with hate, passion with rage, but always controlled, subtle, nuanced.

There were many playwrights who regaled, chilled, or cheered their audiences at this time. Jean-Jacques Bernard (1888–1972), for example, was a practitioner of what came to be known as 'the theatre of silence'. In *Martine* (1922) Bernard did away with psychological analyses, relying on gesture and pauses in the dialogue to emphasise the alteration of emotional situations and to underscore the agony of doubt. The protagonists in *The Cardboard Crown* (*La Couronne de carton*, 1920) and *Leopold the Well-Beloved* (*Léopold le bien-aimé*, 1927), by Jean Sarment (1898–1976), lived in an illusory world, a mirage-dominated realm. *Paquebot Tenacity* (1920) and *Madame Béliard* (1925), by Charles Vildrac, brought sensitive, withdrawn, and poetic people to the stage. The human tragedy inhabiting the lives of these eternal types was emphasised by externalising their deeply buried feelings through seemingly banal conversations.

The facile, supple, and humorous *Tovarich* (1934) of Jacques Deval (1894–1972), won the hearts of audiences the world over. The regional dramas of Marcel Pagnol (1895–1974) – *Marius* (1929), *Fanny* (1931), *Caesar* (1937) – were unforgettable for the reality of the characterisations and the poignant banter of the protagonists.

Violence, cruelty, and a psychoanalytical approach to drama also appeared in boulevard theatre. 'All my plays,' wrote H. R. Lenormand, 'attempt to elucidate the mystery of inner life, to unravel the enigma that man is to himself.'

Introduction

In *Time is a Dream* (*Le Temps est un songe*, 1919), *The Eater of Dreams* (*Le Mangeur de rêves*, 1922), and *Man and his Phantoms* (*L'Homme et ses fantômes*, 1924), Lenormand (1882–1950) brings conflicted, antagonistic and anguished beings to the stage. These Freudian-oriented individuals are haunted by guilt, by repressed and obscure pulsations. Edouard Bourdet (1887–1945), who dug so incisively into the human psyche in *The Prisoner* (*La Prisonnière*, 1926) and *Difficult Times* (*Les Temps difficiles*, 1934), did away with theatrical conventions when he enacted pathological situations on the stage.

There were other playwrights and directors as well, who appeared shortly before World War I and whose creative breadth continued during the interwar period. Not as much appreciated by the majority as were the writers of the boulevard offerings, these highly creative and dedicated workers appealed more directly to an elite – an avant-garde. They questioned, disrupted, toppled the commercially oriented way of doing theatre, which they considered staid and uninspiring.

Jacques Copeau (1879–1949), one of these innovators, struggled valiantly against the business customs and practices of what he considered to be dishonest theatre. Artistry, integrity, and a spirit of renewal reigned in his newly formed theatre du Vieux–Colombier (1913–24) – a theatre he rebuilt from the bottom up along simple classic lines. He did away with the heavy ornamentation, gold plate, and rococo cut-glass chandeliers of the boulevard theatre. He let in clean air where there had been an accumulation of dust and stuffy ideas. He cleansed the theatrical *industry* of all he considered to be cheap and frustrating.

Copeau's Vieux–Colombier theatre was simple in conception and as harmonious as a Doric temple – at once

3

functional, orderly, and beautiful: soft yellow wall panels, green curtains draped back on the side of the stage; indirect lighting soothing to the eyes; a bare stage permitting direct contact between audience and actors. Copeau embodied in the construction of his theatre all that he had assimilated and felt he could use of the ideas of Edward Gordon Craig (1872–1966), who believed the theatre to be an independent entity unto itself; a poetic and suggestive force capable of arresting the quintessential elements of an unfolding drama. From Constantin Stanislavsky (1863–1938), Copeau learned the techniques used in exteriorising a character's inner reality, in acting as an ensemble, and in coordinating every aspect of a production into a unified whole.

Copeau made finished and versatile actors out of the unleavened human talent at his disposal. Prior to the opening of the Vieux–Colombier theatre in Paris, he had his troupe come to the Limon, a country home he rented about an hour from the city by train. There his cast rehearsed out of doors. Stage settings were natural: a tree or flower. Copeau made every demand upon his actors, striving to create vigorous and graceful bodies, as physically adept as those of Elizabethan actors, able to fight, run, perform any arduous leap that a play might require. Louis Jouvet and Charles Dullin, who were members of Copeau's troupe, became masters of their bodies and voices, and of dramatic techniques. Productions of Thomas Heywood's *A Woman Killed with Kindness,* Molière's *The Miser*, Dostoyevky's *The Brothers Karamazov*, Shakespeare's *Twelfth Night*, Claudel's *The Exchange* were made memorable for their artistry and fresh conception. In *The Exchange*, for example, the decor consisted of one tree in the foreground and a black cloth representing the sky; emphasis was thereby focused on the actors' movements and gestures,

4

and on lighting, voice, silences, enhancing the atmosphere of mystery and tension.

In the lengthening shadow of what seemed inevitable war, Jouvet was sent to the front; Copeau joined the auxiliary forces; Dullin, an infantryman, went to Lorraine. Lodged in wet, dirty barracks, often exposed to danger, the three managed to correspond. Copeau was brimming with new ideas. After his demobilisation (1915), Copeau went to Geneva, where he met Emile Jacques-Dalcroze (1865–1950), whose system of eurythmics was enjoying a great vogue. Dalcroze's philosophy was based on the firm belief that actors should learn rhythmic dancing so that they could coordinate bodily movements with speech. Dalcroze introduced Copeau to Adolphe Appia (1862–1928), who stressed the affinities between music and dialogue. Appia championed the creation of a three-dimensional stage; since actors are three-dimensional, he reasoned, so should be the backgrounds they inhabit; these reflect their needs, wants, and personalities and also link them to the time-space factor. Lighting was also vital to performance: it underscored dimensionality, showed up movement, attitude, and gesture. For Appia, lighting was a protagonist, and it became one for Copeau.

In 1917 Copeau and his troupe were sent to New York by the French Ministry of Fine Arts as France's unofficial cultural ambassador of good will. Jouvet and Dullin, both released from the army for medical reasons, joined him. After two arduous years in the United States, producing an incredible number of plays (by Brieux, Hervieu, Rostand, Donnay, Augier, Molière, and others), not always to receptive audiences, Copeau and his troupe returned to Paris. It was then that he founded his school, and, together with Jouvet, created his 'permanent set' at the Vieux-Colombier, the outcome of the work done at the Garrick

Theatre in New York. The permanent set consisted of an architectural whole on the stage which was made up of several levels; there was an arch in the back, stairways on either side, and a projecting apron. It was on this incredibly versatile stage that Copeau created his important productions of plays by Corneille, Maeterlinck, Vildrac, Gide, Romains, Musset, Beaumarchais, Goldoni, and others.

Louis Jouvet (1887–1951) had remained with Copeau for ten years. He referred to himself at the end of this time as a 'valet of the theatre' because he had worked in so many different areas: lighting, staging, carpentry, costume design, and of course, as an actor. In 1923 he accepted the position of director of the Comédie des Champs-Elysées. He not only took over much of Copeau's repertoire, as well as his techniques, but he also added his own rich and inspired vision to the performing arts. His productions of Jules Romains' *Dr. Knock* (1923), Charles Vildrac's *Madame Béliard (1925)*, Bernard Zimmer's *Bava the African* (1926), Jean Sarment's *Leopold the Well-Beloved* (1927), and Marcel Achard's *Jean of the Moon* (1929), to mention but a few, were at once poetic and arresting – simple in concept, a character's truth revealed through the word. Perhaps Jouvet's greatest contributions, however, were his productions of the works of Jean Giraudoux. Had it not been for their collaborative efforts, Giraudoux might have remained the novelist he had been prior to his meeting with Jouvet and not have become one of the most important dramatists of the twentieth century.

Jouvet, a master technician and craftsman, was objective, lucid in his approach to performance. He followed the dictates set forth by Diderot in his *Paradox of the Comedian*. Emotions must be controlled by the actor who incarnates them; they must be defined, delineated with breadth and exactness. A role has to be studied in all of its nuances: gestures, inflections, intonations articulated so that the text may emerge in all of its beauty and grandeur. Audiences are to be inspired by the *word*, the visual image on stage, the breathing they hear, and the emotions conveyed. An actor is to be on a par with the dramatist; that is, his interpretation must be creative. Yet, though fantasy and illusion are not banished from stage life, they must be mastered and directed. Nothing is to be left to chance. Sets, decors, sound effects, vocalisations, costume, lighting, are all to be set down prior to the performance. Like Copeau and Dullin, Jouvet considered the text – language – the play's most important asset. It is through language that great theatre is born. Dullin conveyed his passion for lucre through gesture and facial expression; through a voice that trembled and lips that salivated at the sight of riches; through eyes that glowed with lechery. Jean Vilard (1912–71) also participated in Dullin's troupe. He became director of the Théâtre National Populaire in 1950.

Jean-Louis Barrault (b. 1910) studied with Dullin for four years. He called him 'an aristocrat' of the theatre. From Dullin, Barrault learned the meaning of integrity; a scrupulous awareness of every facet of theatre – each important detail which goes into the creation of a production. It was in 1935, in a mime-drama based on William Faulkner's *As I Lay Dying*, that Barrault made his mark on the theatrical world. His powerful gestural performance, Antonin Artaud suggested, succeeded in organising stage space in an unforgettable manner. As Barrault moved forward on the proscenium, breaking in a wild horse, as he mimed a mother's death agony, controlling his breathing until it became raspy, he shot terror and admiration into the spectators' hearts.

Barrault, who joined the Comédie-Française in 1940, married Madeleine Renaud, already a member of this company, in 1936. Ten years later husband and wife realised a long-cherished dream: they founded their own company, the Théâtre Marigny. Passionate in their devotion to theatre, eclectic in their choice of dramatists, they mounted noteworthy productions of the works of such playwrights as Montherlant, Racine, Molière, Marivaux, Musset, Feydeau, Achard, Sartre, Vauthier, Anouilh, Gide, and Kafka. They also invited directors such as Roger Blin to direct works by Beckett and Genet. It was to Barrault that Claudel entrusted his most personal and poignant play, *Break of Noon* (*Partage de Midi*, 1948); a drama which until this time he had forbad all other directors to produce. Claudel knew that as Dullin's descendent, Barrault would ensure that faith and the work ethic prevailed in his theatre; no concessions to facilitate a production would be made.

Another creative force in the contemporary French theatre was George Pitoëff (1884–1939), the son of a theatrical director. Born and educated in Russia, he worked with Vsevolod Meyerhold (1874–1970) and the stage-set designer Leon Bakst (1866–1924), then with Stanislavsky. His production in St. Petersburg of Chekhov's *Three Sisters* (1912–14), was unforgettable: the decors consisted only of two screens, two lamps, several chairs, and a velvet curtain for a background. The rest of the burden fell upon the actors. In Paris, where he went to study mathematics, architecture, and law, he met his future wife, Ludmilla. Together they founded the Pitoëff Company (1918) and produced such works as Lenormand's *Eater of Dreams* (1922); plays by Claudel, Péguy, and Vitrac; Cocteau's *Orpheus* (1926); and Anouilh's *The Traveller without Luggage* (*Le Voyageur sans bagage*,

1937). Some compared Pitoëff's company to a League of Nations because of the many non-French playwrights that were invited to its stage: Gogol, Andreyev, Gorky, Pushkin, Tolstoy, Seneca, Turgenev, Chekhov, Shaw, Synge, Wilde, Strindberg, Goldoni, Pirandello, Ibsen.

Pitoëff never formulated his dramatic theories in a didactic manner. As was the case for Copeau, Jouvet, and Dullin, the text was uppermost for him. The mise-en-scène emerged directly from the written play and was designed to point up its greatness and concretise its verbal images and rhythms, thus filling the proscenium with electric charges. The director's goal, Pitoëff stated time and time again, was to attempt to understand those forces that had motivated the dramatist to create his work and empowered him to bring forth the creatures of his fantasy. It was on a bare stage, ascetic, monastic in quality, that poetic inspiration resided for Pitoëff – under the magic of the actor's play and the director's design. Influenced by Jacques-Dalcroze, as Copeau had been, Pitoëff accorded great importance to rhythm in fashioning a performance, in fleshing out characters and temperaments. Lighting was also used as a powerful evocative force, playing on backdrops of black, blue, or gray velvet curtains and geometrically conceived decors consisting mainly of a few essential pieces of furniture. A Pitoëff performance was a haunting experience.

Mention must also be made of Gaston Baty (1882–1952), an important director during the interwar period. Collaborator of Firmin Gémier, the actor who had incarnated King Ubu in Jarry's play by that name in 1896, Baty helped create plays by Lenormand, Claudel, Shaw, Crommelynck. In 1923 Baty founded his Compagnons de la Chimère. A disciple of Max Reinhardt (1873–1943), who specialised in mass effects, in mob scenes, using an entire auditorium to create atmosphere, frequently placing audiences within the action itself, Baty also enhanced the role and function of the theatrical director. 'A text cannot say everything,' he wrote. It can convey ideas and emotions, but only to a certain point. Beyond this another zone takes precedence, that of mystery, silence, creating a certain atmosphere and stage climate. The director's task is to bring a whole dimension of unknown forces onto the stage space, thus endowing it with renewed life and vigour. Unlike Copeau, Jouvet and Dullin, Baty attacked 'My Lord, the Word,' in his productions of plays by Musset, Lenormand, Goethe, Shakespeare, Gantillon, and Ansky. His adaptations of Flaubert's *Madame Bovary* (1936) underscored the dreamlike nature of the heroine by creating a flowering and sun-drenched arbour where she was seen walking arm in arm with her lover, enjoying a state of veritable rapture. When despair inundated her world, the lights grew weak and dim; the leaves and flowers, once so brilliant and alive, had withered. (In 1927 Dullin, Pitoëff, Jouvet, and Baty formed a cartel. In *Entr'acte*, the official organ of Jouvet's theatre, they expressed their ideas concerning their aims as directors.)

Michel Saint-Denis must also be included as one of Copeau's heirs. The director of the Compagnie des Quinze (made up of members of Copeau's former troupe), he approached theatre with the same seriousness and intensity as had his master. He imposed upon his troupe a rigorous course of studies which included dance, gymnastics, speech, improvisation, mime, and choral singing. The art of diction took on such musicality and depth that during certain performances it was imbued with unheard of incantatory qualities.

André Obey (1892–1975) offered his new play *Noah* to the Compagnie des Quinze as the opening fare for its first

10

season in 1931 at the Vieux-Colombier. His spiritualised and humanised vision of Noah took on a universal dimension and the religious intensity of medieval miracle plays. Although Obey's Noah was a twentieth-century farmer whose domestic problems were great, his understanding of God and man was archetypal. When, for example, he talked on the phone to God, his metaphysical anguish was so acute that it flowed into the audience.

Dadaists and Surrealists were the descendants of experimental dramatists: Alfred Jarry (*King Ubu*, 1896) and Guillaume Apollinaire (*The Breasts of Tiresias, Les Mamelles de Teresias*, 1917), who had rejected the well-made psychological play as well as romantic and naturalistic dramas with their classical style, their evolving characters, dramatic climaxes, and shattering suspense scenes. Dadaists and Surrealists continued to subvert language and to destroy the logico-Cartesian approach to life and art; by giving precedence to the irrational domain. Tristan Tzara's *The Gas Heart* (*Le Coeur à gaz*, 1920) and Breton and Soupault's *If You Please* (*S'il vous plaît*, 1920), two highly charged and innovative works, conveyed the absurdity, the eroticism of life as they saw it, in cutting, imagistic, and discontinuous dialogue. The hypnotic power of words, the importance of the chance factor in the deployment of repressed emotions, were techniques used by those who sought to unleash unconscious impulses, until now imprisoned, repressed, crushed. The fantastic works of Georges Ribemont-Dessaignes, *The Hangman from Peru* (*Le Bourreau du Pérou*, 1926), Louis Aragon's spirited *The Mirror Wardrobe One Fine Evening* (*L'Armoire à glace un beau soir*, 1924), and Robert Desnos' fantastic *Place de l'Etoile* (1927) are living proof of the untapped and seemingly endless creative élan of these innovators. For Dadaists and

11

Surrealists, dreams were truer than events lived out in the workaday world; and the word, when released automatically from the unconscious, incoherent though it may have seemed to the rationalist, unveiled a whole other dimension. It is this sphere that now took precedence over the cut-and-dry, the predictable and comprehensible workaday reality.

Antonin Artaud (1896–1949), also a Surrealist, was more of a theoretician of the theatre than he was a playwright. After breaking with Breton and his group (1926), he founded The Theatre Alfred Jarry, along with Roger Vitrac and Robert Aron. 'The spectator who comes to us', he wrote in his manifesto concerning his new theatre, 'knows that he has agreed to undergo a true operation, where not only his mind, but his senses and his flesh are going to come into play.' His productions of Vitrac's *The Mysteries of Love* (*Les Mystères de l'amour*, 1927) and *Victor* (1928), as well as some of his own works, made their mark on the avant-garde of his time. Later, in a series of essays he wrote between 1931 and 1935, published in volume form in *The Theatre and its Double* (1938), he outlined his views concerning the creation of a Theatre of Cruelty. Artaud's seminal ideas did much to inspire later playwrights such as Ionesco, Genet, Beckett, Anouilh, and Arrabal.

The Flemish/Belgian dramatists Fernand Crommelynck and Michel de Ghelderode reacted powerfully to the provocative ideas of French playwrights and directors. Although they adhered, at least in name, to the basic theatrical conventions, Crommelynck and Ghelderode transcended them by allowing the domain of the irrational to burst forth onstage. Pain, passion, and rage erupted in all of their grotesque grandeur in such farces as Crommelynck's *The Magnificent Cuckold* (*Le Cocu magnifique*,

1921) and Ghelderode's *Escurial* (1927). The stark nature of these comedies – their violence, shrill antics, and savagely evoked joys and horrors as torrents of love and hatred pour forth from their characters – mark these works with a specially fearful quality, a madness, an expressionism perhaps unique in theatre. Audiences experienced a severe malaise when forced to face the hallucinatory world of Crommelynck and Ghelderode: delirious domains where burlesque and sensuality vie with the occult, sadomasochism walks arm in arm with heartfelt piety, and the macabre blends with the priapic.

More conventional than the works of the Dadaists and Surrealists or the Flemish/Belgian dramatists are the mythically oriented works of Cocteau, Giraudoux, Anouilh, and Claudel. Dramatising original experiences, often transcendental rather than personal, Cocteau's *Orpheus* (1926), Giraudoux's *Ondine (1939)* and *The Madwoman of Chaillot* (*La Folle de Chaillot*, 1945), Anouilh's *The Traveller Without Luggage* (1937) and *The Thieves' Carnival* (*Le Bal des voleurs*, 1938), Claudel's *Break of Noon*, written in 1905, but officially performed only in 1948, are unsettling: they question, triturate, pain and render jubilant – but always in a subtle, nuanced, and sensitive manner. Their characters are recognisable; their sequences, relatively rational, certainly logical by comparison with the dramas of the Dadaists and Surrealists. Their dialogue, poetic, doleful, and poignant at times searing, speaks to the heart as well as the mind. Theirs is a theatre of all time, of all place, Everyman's.

Dramatists, directors, and actors between World Wars I and II gave form to what had existed in the vague no-man's-land of untried formulas. They brought integrity, sacrifice, and beauty to their artistic creations, gave eter-

13

nity to a new brand of theatre. Each in his own way learned how to convey and instill raw pain and brutality as well as jubilation and tenderness – pointing up the serenity and poetry that accompany real love, and the grotesque and sublime in flights of fantasy or terror, be they deeply spiritual, sexual, or a fusion of both.

PART I

DADA, SURREALISM, AND THE THEATRE OF CRUELTY

Tristan Tzara, the father of Dada, André Breton, the creator of Surrealism, Roger Vitrac, who shared their views, and Antonin Artaud, who brought forth the Theatre Alfred Jarry and the Theatre of Cruelty, were seminal forces in twentieth-century theatre. They were not, except perhaps for Vitrac, great playwrights; they were visionaries. They fed the world with new ideas and provocative sensations; they opened up the unconscious for artists to peer into, to experience. Later twentieth-century dramatists, such as Jean Genet, Eugene Ionesco, Samuel Beckett, Fernando Arrabal, and Jean Vauthier, consciously or unconsciously were inspired by the flamboyant and provocative writings of Tzara, Breton, Vitrac, and Artaud. Thanks to them to a great extent, twentieth-century theatre reached new heights and memorable dimensions.

15

Dada, the term around which Tzara and his friends were to group themselves, spelled a fresh approach to life, a brushing aside of all that was secure, permanent, consistent, predictable. Dadaists opted for the unconventional and the absurd – notions that would endow humanity with new, colourful, and ground-breaking vision. Tzara's brash and anarchic views crashed into the placid Swiss city of Zurich like a meteor. He sought successfully to scandalise its staid bourgeois society, appealing powerfully to young and creative-minded natives and foreigners who understood the *absurdity* and incongruity of life and the hypocritical, superficial values dominating ruling groups everywhere. To grasp the meaning of the rebellion waged by the Dadaists and the reasons compelling them to give vent to their feelings of disgust with a civilisation in its twilight stages, one must take into consideration the emotional climate of the time. Many young people considered World War I a false war, a pointless slaughter intended to further the bourgeois way of life, which was not theirs and which they believed was useless and detrimental to the creative spirit. When Dadaism was born, the war was dragging on and on, and the end was not in sight. Deaths were mounting, disease and suffering in the trenches were unspeakably harsh. Only by rooting out the causes and the climate which paved the way for such a massacre could another approach to life be forthcoming. Instead of death, the Dadaists clamoured for life; sincerity, rather than hypocrisy. No longer would they give credence to notions such as honour, motherland or fatherland, morality, family, art, religion, liberty, fraternity, and all the other values so lauded by a world they knew to be structured on shaky if not rotten foundations. To re-examine the groundbed of their society, to re-evaluate the pillars upon which it was so solidly anchored, is what they intended to accomplish, but they had to destroy these things first.

André Breton had been intrigued by Tzara and Dada-ism. He took an active part in their demonstrations in 1919, attempting thereby to free himself from the overpowerful mantle of society. By 1921, however, Breton had grown weary of Tzara's nihilism. He found his emphasis on negation to be unproductive and equally as systematic as the way of life he was trying to annihilate. Dadaism no longer answered Breton's intellectual or emotional needs. He sought a more positive and more creative stand. Having worked in psychiatric hospitals and studied Freud's writ-ings, Breton was fascinated with the unconscious as a storehouse of infinite riches – for the poet, the artist, all creative people. He set forth his ideas in three *Surrealist Manifestos* (1924, 1930, 1934), rejecting in a structured way both the negativism of Dada and the rational civilisa-tion of the West which had given birth to World War I, to a society that encouraged a routine and limited view of existence. Surrealism offered a positive credo: to delve into the unconscious meant to discover a new world, the fruits of which would trigger tremulous mysteries, diverse forms. Surrealism, Breton suggested, was *a way of life*. It brought forth the allure of everything that erupted from the subliminal realm. This material was believed to be endowed with a 'special light' which Breton called 'the *light* of the image, which scintillates, sparks, and gives rise to further conflagrations which the poet may apprehend.'[1] The images that come into view may guide the poet like glistening stars on a black night; they may be landmarks, helping him to capture and verbalise what he so frantically searches for in that obscure and haunting – but amorphous – inner realm.

Breton rejected moral commitments to a society he detested; he disallowed compromise and those whose lives were regulated by this principle. The fortuitous, the chance factor, coincidence, the dream, all paved the way for a deeper reality to be unearthed, the *real* world to be glimpsed. It is through the unconscious and its infinite emanations that the creative individual is invited to penetrate the bizarre, unusual, grotesque, and sublime – that exhilarating world of unknown quantities where 'the marvellous is always beautiful. . .'[2] So, too is the imagination beautiful, elusive, and alluring: a faculty Breton refers to as the 'beloved', because it does not adapt to routine, mundane existence, but encourages the greatest mental freedom.

As Dadaism had opened a door in its time, so Surrealism was to follow suit. Rather than remaining stationary at the threshold, as had the Dadaists, the Surrealists advanced into the room, explored its every nook and cranny, and returned with the poem, the painting, the piece of music. 'Hordes of words,' undiluted and unvitiated, cascaded forth when Breton plumbed his depths. It was these verbal ejaculations that made for the innovative quality of so many of his works: *The Lost steps* (*Les Pas perdus*, 1924), *Nadja* (1928), and more.

Surrealism was both negative and positive: rejecting outworn and ossified values and ways of replacing these through the discovery of new, mobile, and strikingly different poetic processes. As Einstein had brought fresh insights into the scientific scheme of things and Freud, into the psychoanalytical field, so Breton and his friends – Aragon, Eluard, Péret, and others – were to explore the unconscious as manifested in a variety of domains: insanity, humour, the grotesque, the marvellous, the gratuitous – and play. Their goal was to transcend the usual deductive, inductive and reductive procedures, so that they could reach into their primordial depths and bring back the riches they discovered there to the workaday world. Hypnosis was also to become a formidable technique used by Breton, Desnos, Crevel, and others to forge ahead into mysterious climes peopled by terrifying and also loving shades and specters. These psychic explorers were also assiduous practitioners of dream narration as a mental phenomenon – not to be associated with spiritualism. Aragon even suggested, perhaps in jest, that such practices had given rise to 'an epidemic of sleepers' among poets bent upon discovering the new by regressing into the past.[3]

Roger Vitrac, a Dadaist and Surrealist for a time, was the author of *Victor*, a play which earned virtually no recognition when first performed in 1928 but attracted accolades when directed by Jean Anouilh in 1962. The finest example of Surrealist theatre, it used the dream as a dramatic vehicle, combining with it farce, the gratuitous act, and tragedy. It sought successfully to dislocate and torture language, as Tzara and Breton had done before, but now with greater intellectuality and dramatic impact. *Victor* is both painful and satiric; on stage audiences are exposed to the most preposterous of situations, characterisations, and gestural sequences, clothed in a combination of low- and highbrow humour – black humour!

Antonin Artaud, the founder of the Theatre Alfred Jarry and the Theatre of Cruelty, is considered today as one of the great theorists on theatre in the twentieth century. A visionary and mystic, he saw the theatre as had the people of antiquity, as a ritual able to give rise to a religious experience within actor and audience. To achieve such a goal, Artaud sought to expand the spectator's reality by arousing the explosive and creative forces within his unconscious, an area he considered more powerful than the rational conscious in determining an individual's actions. By means of a theatre based on myths, symbols, and gestures, Artaud whipped up irrational forces that turned a collective dramatic event into a personal and living experience.

1
Tristan Tzara
(1896—1963)

'The theatre. Since it still remains attached to a romantic imitation of life, to an illogical fiction, let us give it all the natural vigor it had to begin with – let it be amusement or poetry,' wrote Tristan Tzara, the founder of Dada and author of *The Gas Heart*.[1] A movement designed to destroy the values and standards of European bourgeois society, Dada, as conveyed in Tzara's *First Manifesto* (1916), represented negation, a rebellion against the political, economic, and social systems believed to be responsible for the 'outrage' that was World War I. Dada also rejected all forms of accepted art, advocating anti-representationalism, anti-literary procedures, anti-logical sequences and patterns of thought, anti-syntactical structures and semantic valuations. When summing up his movement, Tzara wrote: 'Dada signifies nothing'. He then set down the following equations: 'order=disorder; I=non I; affirmation=negation; if each one says the contrary it's because he is right.'[2]

Tzara, whose real name was Sami Rosenstock, was born in Moinesti, Rumania. He studied at the University of

Zurich, and it is in this city also, so it had been claimed, that he played chess with the exiled Lenin. Here, too, he founded Dada on 8 February 1916, at 6.00 p.m. at the Cafe Terrasse in Zurich, Switzerland. Together with his friends Hugo Ball, a German revolutionary emigre, Richard Huelsenbeck, also a German, but adhering to a more politically oriented path, and Hans Arp, the Alsatian painter, Tzara played his part in giving birth to something so new and so different as to be shocking and thrilling. But how did they come upon the name Dada? Fortuitously. They opened up the Larousse dictionary at random and on a randomly chosen word placed a paper cutter which pointed to another word: *dada*. This word was defined as 'hobby horse' and as 'father' in baby language; as a fad or pet obsession and also as 'yes' in Russian. What was of import to Tzara and his friends, however, was not the dictionary meaning, because this smacked of the very logical and rational system they sought to destroy. For them, *dada* implied the emergence of a new, spontaneous, impermanent vision, the reign of the chance factor: the passage from non-being to being.

To these ends, Tzara, Ball, Huelsenbeck, and the Rumanian painter, Marcel Janco, organised their first manifestation in Zurich at the Cabaret Voltaire on 30 March 1916. On this occasion, they devoted their energies to anti-literary procedures: the simultaneous recitation of poems by Tzara, Huelsenbeck, and Janco, thereby preventing listeners from understanding a word that was being said and doing away with the very notion of *lecture* and *rational* comprehension.

Tzara's earliest dramatic work, *The First Celestial Adventure of Mr. Antipyrine* (1916), was in keeping with Dada dicta. It was highly unconventional, and for the outsider, completely nonsensical. 'Mr. Antipyrine's Manifesto,' published as part of the play and read by Tzara at Salle Waag in Zurich on Bastille Day, 14 July 1916, espoused 'incoherent spontaneity' as a literary technique. It championed an unleashing of unconscious contents – a creative process devoid of logic and celebration. Cartesian and Euclidean thought processes had to be banished, along with rules and regulations – since these foster a climate of rigidity. Advocated, too, were perpetual mobility and detachment, thus paving the way for an explosive, intensely original experience.

Tzara's assault on western civilisation pursued its vigorous course in his seven Manifestos. For him writing meant a re-kindling of the ancient magic which words originally possessed, a reawakening of their ritualistic and incantatory power. To effect such transformation required a whole new frame of reference: an intellectual and emotional climate which would open up the senses and allow inner vision to flow outward, thus encouraging instincts to dilate. What society had suffocated and virtually extinguished in the personality of the artist, Tzara would now release. Words as used by conventional writers had grown hollow and stale during the past centuries. To bring forth fresh meanings and arouse different sensations necessitated a destruction of the old. Tzara used the very instruments and techniques of traditional writers to effect the wanted change: repetition, enumeration, listings, but under Tzara's baton words were juxtaposed in seemingly meaningless sequences. Nouns were piled up but were unrelated, as were adjectives and adverbs; letters were joined in clusters that were not words. Tzara thereby did away with normal syntactical structure, with logic and semantic order.

Tzara's *Second Dada Manifesto*, held in Meise Hall in Zurich on 23 March 1918, launched a frontal attack on outworn notions concerning the work of art. Art was not to be looked upon as a celebration, nor were stylistic schools to be tolerated, be they Fauve, Cubist, or Futurist – or any other. One must not codify what is fluid or stratify what continually alters in consistency, he contended, but rather create an individual vision born of one's own imagination. Modes of thought and modes in art cannot but 'betray' the life experience, nor must the creative person accept compromise as a way out of a dilemma. He urged that a new language be found, empowering the writer to purify the word and thus create concrete, visceral images instead of the vacuous abstractions used by the popular writers of the time. 'Thought is made in the mouth', he contended: any kind of thinking process or intervention of the rational function is a 'lie', for it undermines the individual's chaotic inner forces, which lie smoldering in his depths. Nor did Tzara believe in the notion of progress: a cornerstone of western thought and religion. Such a doctrine, and its doctrinaires, stamps a certain meaning on the world and the universe which is not only erroneous but cruel, for it gives people false hopes. Hope of any kind is devoid of meaning: it is artificial, superfluous, and illusory.

'Spontaneous incoherence', the dislocation of language, the expressing and conveying of ideas through scandalous demonstrations and other forms of provocation – these were to be Tzara's techniques for overthrowing the blind routines in which western culture was so deeply entrenched. He urged that every individual shout out his or her needs and opinions because 'there is a great destructive and negative job to be done. Sweep out, mop up.'[3]

Tzara arrived in Paris in 1919. He was warmly greeted by André Breton and his friends Louis Aragon, Philippe Soupault, and others. Very much in awe of Tzara and his activities, Breton joined forces with him, and together they pursued the same tactics in the French city as Tzara had in the Swiss. The Grand Palais des Champs-Elysées was the locus of Tzara's *Fourth Manifesto*; 5 February 1919, was the date. During the course of this meeting, Tzara called his audience 'idiots' and delivered other verbal assaults that mystified, irritated, and disturbed his eager listeners.

Tzara urged that the fortuitous take precedence in a creative work and gave his recipe for the writing of a Dada poem.

> Take a newspaper. Take some scissors. Pick out an article which is as long as you wish your poem to be. Cut out the article. Then cut out carefully each of the words in the article and put them in a bag. Shake gently. Then take out each piece one after the other. Copy them down conscientiously in the order in which they left the bag. The poem will resemble you and you will find yourself to be an infinitely original writer with a charming sensitivity even though you will not be understood by the vulgar.[4]

When audiences expected a literary discussion at the Palais des Fêtes on 23 January 1920, Tzara again resorted to provocation. He announced he would recite some verses, but instead took out a newspaper and began reading the first article that came into view to the accompaniment of bells and rattles. The audience began whistling, catcalling, and shouting threats. To add fire to fury, Francis Picabia, one of the earliest exponents of Dada in painting, exhibited some of his shockingly different canvases.

Despite Tzara's negativism, expressed in such works as *25 Poems* (1918), *7 Dada Manifestos* (1916–20), *The Approximate Man and Other Writings* (1930), *The Anti-head* (1933), *Grains and By-Products* (*Grains et issues*, 1939), he conveyed a whole 'human experience' and a 'metaphysics'.[5] In fact, his preoccupation with the deeper meanings of life was uppermost; otherwise he would not have attempted to destroy what he felt impeded its ebullience, its free-flowing and highly creative quality, nor would his approach have been so violent and vituperative. His nihilistic view, which precluded any kind of passivity, encouraged him to be destructive but not to resort to armed conflict; the 'auto-devouring' society which had brought civilisation to its downfall had to be cut from within, reconstituted, so that each individual could *really* discover his place within society, within the universe.

Theatre for Tzara was neither a spectacle nor an amusement nor a pastime. It was designed, as were other Dada works, to provoke, to shock people out of their customary lethargy. Sets, costumes, language, theatrical conventions in general, and the well-made play (with its psychological analyses, plots, characterisations, conflicts, and logical or emotional buildups of tension) were all rejected.

Tzara's plays, *The First Celestial Adventure of Mr. Antipyrine* and *The Second Celestial Adventure of Mr. Antipyrine*, use sounds, accumulation of images, reiterated phrases, disconnected or catalogue-style sequences of words, enumerations of unrelated objects and images, and other seemingly nonsensical verbal arrangements, as a scenario. The fortuitous dominates; spontaneity is the rule of the game. Some critics have suggested that 'love and life' are the themes of these plays; and believe that tension and conflict in a nonclassical sense exist in them. Violent language, fervour, eroticism, and a bent for the macabre are inherent in Tzara's dramatic world.[6]

Everything about Tzara's theatre was different. The characters, although given names (Mr. Pipi, the Pregnant Woman, Mr. Bleubleu, Mr. Cricri), were not flesh and blood; rather, as their names indicate, they represented certain realities, which only readers of the plays could appreciate. For theatregoers, unaware of their appellations, they remained anonymous voices. In any case, they were devoid of any real individuality. As for many of the conversations between the protagonists, they were for the most part incomprehensible, pointing once again to the truth of Tzara's statement as it appeared in the 'Manifesto for Mr. Antipyrine': 'Art isn't serious, I assure you.'[7]

As Mr. Antipyrine, played by André Breton, spoke out his assonanced, incoherent, and rhythmic sonorities, he settled and unsettled the nerves of his listeners, 'soco bgaï affahou/zoumbaï zoumbaï zoumbaï zoum.' The Pregnant Woman, enacted by Cécile Arnauld, invoked her strangely juxtaposed consonants and vowels in vocalised speech, 'toudi-a-voua/soco bgaï affahou.' When Mr. Bleubleu, portrayed by Philippe Soupault, chimed in 'borkou mmbaz gymanstic mmbaz 20785,' the concert seemed complete.[8] What might have sounded devoid of meaning for some may indeed have had significance for others. Let us recall that at the time Tzara and some of his friends had a profound feeling for African art, as had the Cubists before them. A character in Tzara's play, for example, sported the African name Npala Garroo. It has been suggested that some of the dialogue was a phonetic transcription of refrains from certain African poems Tzara was translating at the time.

Tzara's *Second Celestial Adventure of Mr. Antipyrine*, performed on 26 May, although armed with incoherencies, sported a theme. The characters were still mere voices, brought into being so that statements could be exchanged, thus providing dialogue; but a more despairing note was injected into the images. Still, the entire venture seemed to have been constructed in keeping with Tzara's recipe for poetry-making: clipping words from newspapers, shaking them up in a hat, withdrawing them, and pasting them together in a kind of collage or catalogue.

The Ear (played by Breton), the Disinterested Brain (Ribemont-Dessaigne), Mr. Absorption (Eluard), and Mr. Antipyrine (Aragon) utter their verbiage (verbs, adjectives, nouns, sounds, irrational formulas, rhythms) in a further attempt to discredit rational sequences and conventional processes of language as a means of communication, particularly in theatre. The game-like nature of the dialogue divests the work of suspense and empathy – certainly of anything that comes close to Aristotelian purgation. The chance factor dominates; entrances and exits seem pointless. Sounds are repeated, as are letters, in rhythmic sequences ('tzaca tzac tzaca tzac tzaca tzac tzaca tzac') underscoring a certain musicality; definite and indefinite articles are omitted, juxtapositions replace subordinate clauses. Since all parts of the sentences or each of the words within them have seemingly similar value, it is up to the reader or viewer to form his or her own associations and responses. The author, then, imposes no point of view, nor do relationships come into being between protagonists; sounds, images, and sensations are the only elements of importance, and these bombard readers or spectators alike. Since little or no punctuation is included in the text, the actors reading their parts decide where they will breathe, in keeping with their emotional needs and reactions. The costumes were fascinating: 'Phantasmal beings dressed in black paper, with white cardboard cowls for headgear, line up on the platform. Their orchestra leader is better adorned; his cowl is an expressive face on which are stuck a box of *Luculus* noodles and a gray-gloved hand.'[10]

The First Adventure was considered a spoof, a humourous and musing interlude. Not so with the second. The insults leveled at the audience – or so they thought – warranted a counter-attack. The well known Salle Gaveau concert hall, where the dramatic performance was held, was the seat of scandalous goings on. During the interval, it seems that some in the audience went out to purchase meat and other provisions, which they hurled at the performers during the course of the proceedings. They, too, felt the urge to express their annoyance.

'The Gas Heart' (1920)

The Gas Heart, considered the masterpiece of Dada theatre, was performed at the Galerie Montaigne in Paris on 10 June 1921. What makes this play unique is its cast of characters. Each protagonist is an organ of the face: Ear, played by Soupault; Mouth, performed by Ribemont-Dessaignes; Eye, portrayed by Aragon; Neck, by Benjamin Péret.[11] Provocative as always, Tzara's bent for surprise, his desire to demolish routine and structured ways, reached a fascinating level in *The Gas Heart*, perhaps going so far as to inspire Samuel Beckett to create his *Not I*, a play in which only red lips are visible on a blackened stage – lips that move as they relate the story of a seventy-year-old woman.

New spatial concepts were also in the offing in *The Gas Heart*. Ear, Mouth, Eye, and Neck all live in space: they are there, present. They also exist in time: stage time, vanishing after the performance is over. Tzara introduces a variety of time and space concepts in his play with such words as 'chronometer', 'needle', 'tic-tac' and 'organised time', deriding in this fashion society's emphasis on the regularity of sequential moments. For Tzara, linear (clock) time kills beauty, destroys what lives cyclically in the imagination or in subliminal spheres. He delighted in mythical time, that of the dream; enjoyed by the primitives and by truly creative people.

Just as the Cubists, namely Picasso and Braque, had broken up flat planes and had fragmented what was formerly considered whole (the body, the face), so *The Gas Heart* cut and broke down the world of appearances by using a novel cast of characters in new situations and relationships: Ear speaks to Eye, to Mouth, and so forth. No longer a slave of western logic, Tzara's characters have the faculty to move about, to breathe, to shout, and to relate or not relate to other parts of the face. Tzara's attempt to rid himself of the patterns set down so rigidly by western *logos* calls to mind the Zen Buddhists, who created the *koan*: a subject given to the student by the master for meditative purposes; a non-rational paradoxical theme which would test his spiritual and intuitive powers, help him transcend self-consciousness, and induce heightened self-awareness and cosmic consciousness. Through association, suggestion, elaboration, and of course the spontaneous or intuitive factors which created his arresting crystalline images in the play, Tzara succeeded in recovering what had been repressed in the individual.

Tzara's stage directions serve to create an atmosphere of make-believe and ebullience; they also determine geometric and choreographic relationships between the character-organs. 'Neck is above the stage. Nose facing him above the public. All other characters enter and leave *ad libitum*.'[12]

Since Neck stands above the stage and above Nose, it transcends the action. Nose, opposite the audience and facing Neck, represents a kind of go-between or mediating entity, an objective critic of what is taking place onstage. Both Nose and Neck are detached from the conflict they see before them; they only observe and comment upon it.

Tristan Tzara

Tzara's seemingly senseless verbiage, the comings and goings onstage which appear to be directed by the chance factor, do have satiric intent and bring to mind Ionesco's *The Bald Soprano* (*La Cantatrice Chauve*, 1953) and *The Future Is In the Eggs* (*L'Avenir est dans les oeufs*, 1958), among other works. The words and listings Tzara heaped one upon the other, creating a pseudo monotonous and formula-like style, are surprisingly meaningful and rational.

MOUTH: The conversation is getting dull, isn't it?
EYE: Yes, isn't it.
MOUTH: Very dull, isn't it?
EYE: Yes, isn't it?
MOUTH: Naturally, isn't it?
EYE: Evidently, isn't it?
MOUTH: Dull, isn't it?

Such banalities, repeated as they are in and out of context, also bring to mind Pinter at his best – *The Dumb Waiter, The Birthday Party, The Caretaker* – eliciting, as he does, through duplication, silence, sarcasm, and *non-sequiturs*, the most profound and poignant laughter.

That Tzara chose organs of the head as his protagonists indicated his interest in realigning what most people believe to be separate or set functions. He did not encourage Eye simply to see, or Ear just to hear. These strict confines were no longer valid for the Dadaists. The Symbolists had had recourse to the literary device of *synesthesia* to transcend the limiting views of western logicians. For them also, the Eye could hear, the Ear could see, and so forth. In focusing on the head, indicating a desire to alter and expand its functions, Tzara might have been saying that unlike the primitive, who lives in close relationship with nature and himself, the so-called civilised

31

person is cut off from the world around him and exists only peripherally in loneliness and despair.

The characters in *The Gas Heart*, as physiological entities, are both autonomous and linked to the rest of the corpus – to the vital organ in particular: the Gas Heart. The heart, as the centering force, the catalyst, propels all the other elements involved. It suffers and loves. Nor does it remain still on stage. It walks slowly, circulating about just as the real heart pumps the blood throughout the body, visiting the appendages so as to keep them going. An instrument which insures life, the heart in Tzara's play also has contemporary ramifications: like a car or other moving vehicle, it is gas-fed, indicating its machine-like quality and its role as a symbol of the new society based on mass production, speed, and noise.

Is there a plot to *The Gas Heart?* Yes, so to speak. In Act I we learn from the very outset that Mouth and Eye are a couple; we are also told in innocuous sequences of words, reminiscent of a ritual chant, about the joy, irritation, and passion Ear and Mouth feel for each other. When Mouth exits, Eye is depressed. From Ear we learn that Eye has told Mouth to open her mouth 'for the candy of the eye', implying that Eye loves Mouth and wants to devour her. We also deduce from the dialogue that Eye is masculine and Mouth feminine. Eye continues to express his passion for Mouth in blatant and mechanical terms, comparing her facial beauty to a 'precision chronometer'. Ear goes on to explain the ramifications of this remark, including the possibility of Mouth being cold. Eye pursues his courtship: with the entrance of a new character, Clytemnestra, he hopes to make Mouth jealous. Ear intuits the difficult relationship in the offing, since Clytemnestra is a married woman. He trembles at the thought of the imbroglio to come. Mouth, annoyed by Eye's passionate outbursts, wants 'to turn off the tap'. She leaves. Suspense, similar to that aroused in a soap opera, invades the stage space. Nose, Eyebrow, and Eye pursue a never-lagging conversation, grinding out their fierce anger against an industrialised society.

In Act II we discover that Clytemnestra is a horse, and Mouth, therefore, must also be one. In fact, the two are really one person. The conversation, still revolving around love, is carried on in racing language. Eye speaks of 'amorous jostlings' and pursues his courtship. Mouth announces that she has won a lot of money at the races and is thrilled about it, expressing her pleasure in watery terms: swimming in a fountain with necklaces of goldfish. She also mentions the fact that a young man followed her in the street on a bicycle. At this point, Eye's emotions flare. He castigates her for being so unfeeling. Mouth exits. Pain and pathos are evident, although smothered in *non sequiturs*. Eye, however, waxes lyrical again in a kind of musical verbal interlude. Only at the end of the act does Eyebrow scream 'Fire! Fire!', implying that the passion experienced by Eye has ignited and can no longer be contained.

In Act III Neck uses the all-important symbol of the 'sewing-machine,' representative of the feminine element, to indicate Mouth's decision to marry Eye. Nose and Neck attack her for yielding to what they consider to be an illusory condition of marital bliss. Despite the reprimands, Mouth will maintain her ways, her individuality, her ideas. She knows the meaning of love and is loved. She personifies the Dada view of Aphrodite, which may have nothing to do with the image projected on this feminine form by the Greeks.

Finally Eye declares once again his passion for Mouth, who is also Clytemnestra. Despite Mouth's many refusals and departures, and Eye's despair, all ends well. Ear discovers that his horse has won; moments later, Mouth enters on all fours only to find Eye also on all fours. 'It will conclude with a lovely marriage', the members of the cast repeat one at a time; then, with *brio,* they tell the audience it is time to go home and to bed.

Tzara's play is anti-dramatic for those who do not wish to penetrate its automatic language, its feelings or thoughts. The images, alliterations, rhymes, echoes, not only lend rhythmic value to the lines but also amplitude to the poetry. No matter how skimpy the plot may be, it is there, as are characterisations, be they human or animal. Important, too, are the free associations which the images trigger in the imagination of the audience and protagonists. Beautiful and banal, repulsive and attractive, morose and optimistic, in their own hilarious or mocking way Tzara's statements do evoke emotion.

When it was first performed *The Gas Heart* was considered a defiant venture destined to alienate audiences, to break conventional ties of communication. The second time it was produced (1923), it was part of an evening's entertainment which included music by Auric, Milhaud, Satie, and Stravinsky; poems by Apollinaire, Cocteau, Eluard, and Tzara; films by Man Ray and Hans Richer; speeches by Ribemont-Dessaignes and others. The fact that *The Gas Heart* was produced by professionals and semi-professionals this second time (it was directed by Yssia Siderski, and the sets were done by N. Ganovsky, the costumes by Sonia Delaunay-Terck and Victor Barthe) really violated the spirit of Dada. Breton and his friend felt that since the play had been previously performed its shock value no longer existed.

The Gas Heart had just started when Breton walked onto the stage and began hitting one of the actors with a cane;

apparently he broke his arm. Breton, Aragon, and Péret, who had joined in the melée, were soon thrown out. Eluard, who continued the battle, was asked to leave. The actors were unable to fight back since their roles required them to be incarcerated in cardboard boxes. The result: everything onstage was in shambles. Only Marcel Duchamps' 'Bicycle Wheel', which had been placed on a kitchen stool, remained intact.[13] Tzara, who sued for damages in a conventional bourgeois court proceeding, won his case.

Tzara's *The Gas Heart* follows the iconoclastic traditions started by Jarry's *King Ubu* and Apollinaire's *The Breasts of Tiresias*. It reaches out still further, however, and thrashes more brashly everything that smacks of establishment. Its linguistic gyrations, its anti-logos, its shedding of grammatical and semantic ties, invite audiences and readers alike to experience brilliant yet disconnected images, alluring for their visual interest, their hypnotic power, and their lulling or staccato rhythms. Like a film strip, these images pass in review with great speed, dizzying those who attempt to visualise them all. These kaleidoscopic collages, as they may be called, or fragmented instanteous visualisations, are innovative and certainly were instrumental – consciously or not – in the development of Ionesco's anti-theatre and in the creation of some of Beckett's short pieces (his halting dialogue in *The Play* and other works), his organic and eviscerated characters, and their simultaneous speeches. So, too, did Pinter and Pinget benefit from Tzara's verbal gymnastics, his satiric and nerve-benumbing theatrical homilies.

Dada's official demise is said to have occurred in May 1921, when the students at the School of Fine Arts drowned its effigy in the Seine. Tzara's enormous spirit of revolt, his need to replace logical reason with deliberate madness, to create chaos where cosmos supposedly reigned, to foment riots and concoct hoaxes, did its part to squash complacency and encourage a spirit of doubt and fresh investigations into the creative principle. As Tzara wrote in his Dada *Manifesto* of 1918, 'Art is a private thing, the artist makes it for himself; a comprehensible work is a product of journalism.'[14]

2
André Breton
(1896–1966)

If You Please (1920), written by André Breton and his poet-novelist friend Philippe Soupault (1897–), is one of the earliest examples of automatic writing in theatre. This technique is defined by Breton as follows: 'Pure psychic automatism by means of which it is hoped to express, either verbally or in writing, or in another manner, the real functioning of thought. Dictation of thought, in the absence of all control exercised by reason, outside of all aesthetic and moral preoccupation.'[1] By freeing the unconscious of all restraints imposed upon it by society – the arbiter of logic, aesthetics, and ethics – consciousness is bypassed; words and images flow freely into the manifest world. Although not everything emerging from the subliminal world is worthy of inclusion in a play or poem, Breton considered it an ever-productive, virtually infallible source of riches and suggested that if the writer were not satisfied with the word, clause, sentence, or visualisation first transcribed, surely the next sequences would be of higher quality.[2]

During their seances of automatic writing, Breton and Soupault were both fascinated by the ease with which quantities of words leaped into existence – untouched, unhampered, and unvitiated by the logical, rational mind. Breton referred to himself and to Soupault, along with other surrealists (Pierre Reverdy, Robert Desnos, and more) who practiced automatic writing, as transcribers of information secreted by the unconscious. No intervention of the thinking function was to be applied; no 'evaluation' of 'filtration' on the part of the author would be exercised. Breton and Soupault, with pen in hand, listened in rapt excitement to what they alluded to as their 'spoken thought'. They were for all intents and purposes 'receptacles of so many echoes, modest *recording machines* of a deeper reality.'[3] It is from this layer within the unconscious that the sibylline pronouncements of the surreal catapulted forth, to be incorporated in *If You Please*.

Breton, born in Normandy and brought up at Saint-Brieux, opted for a medical career. He spent much of World War I in the artillery, which was at the time part of the Health Service, and was shocked and emotionally scathed by the suffering he saw in the hospitals. He therefore took particular umbrage at what he considered to be the hollow patriotic verbiage uttered by men of letters such as Barrès, Bergson, and Claudel. They had never known front-line fighting, the difficult conditions of trench warfare, the cruelty, the pain experienced by soldiers. He did, however, admire Guillaume Apollinaire, the leader of the literary avant-garde at the time; and Jacques Vaché (1885–1919), poet and student of fine arts, for his supreme detachment blended with acerbic jocularity.

In 1917 Apollinaire introduced Breton to Philippe Soupault and soon afterward to Louis Aragon. Two years later Breton and his new friends founded a journal, sarcastically named *Littérature* (1919–24), which published some works by such heteroclite authors as Gide, Valéry, Apollinaire, and Lautréamont.

Quite knowledgeable in things psychological, Breton began investigating some of the inner meanings of his visions and reveries. On one occasion, just before falling asleep, an image of 'a man cut in two by the window' leapt into existence and others followed. He transcribed these visualisations which raced past his mind's eye (onto paper), and then transformed them into poems and theatre pieces. What the psychoanalyst sought to discover in his patient, using Freudian methods of association, hypnosis, and other techniques, Breton had effected gratuitously. He and Soupault then decided to collaborate on the first surrealistic work, *The Magnetic Fields* (*Les Champs magnétiques*, 1919). It consisted of sequences of dialogue, each speaker pursuing his unconscious pulsations, disregarding formalities and obligations owed the other. Words were endowed with their own creative energy, each possessed its own pulse and heartbeat, thought, emotion, and feeling tones; it was a microcosm and as such was endowed with unlimited polarities – everything existing within it, the substantial and the amorphous, the fluid and the fixed. It was through the word, a concrete yet paradoxically formless entity, that the dull façades of western life, and their corresponding religious, political, and aesthetic institutions might be pierced to disclose new, alluring, and forbidden zones. In this spirit of investigation of the surreal, Breton and Soupault wrote *If You Please*; and in so doing, discovered the 'marvellous' world that lies just beyond the reach of the rational.

'If You Please' (1920)

If You Please, first performed on 27 March at the Salle Berlioz in Paris, was part of a larger programme which included Tzara's *The First Celestial Adventure of Mr. Antipyrine*. Breton and Soupault both acted in their drama, as did Mlle L. Moton, Paul and Gala Eluard, Theodore Fraenkel, Henry Cliquennois, and Georges Ribemont-Dessaignes.[4]

Although Breton and Soupault brought forth their Surrealist theatrical piece in the spirit of automatism and willful suspension of critical faculties, one may harbour serious doubts as to the extent of the freedom exercised in the writing of this anti-play. *If You Please* has characters and plot; it builds tension of sorts. Certainly the authors must have selected the images used, rejecting what would have made for monotony; they probably had some direction in mind when they set down their automatically received dialogue. Dislocation of syntax and semantic notions; omission of causal links between clauses, sentences, and images; and stream-of-consciousness associations are present, but they have been fashioned to underscore the colourful and heteroclite nature of this intriguing theatrical work. That the play is divided into conventional acts is a mockery of traditional theatre since the sequences are unrelated one to the other, underscoring the artificiality of the techniques used in the so-called 'well-made play'.

Act I takes place in a drawing room furnished in the conventional manner: armchairs, a cassock, a low table, a lamp, mirrors, a window, and a door. The forty-year-old Paul, sporting an 'American style moustache' stoops a bit when kissing then confessing his passionate love for the twenty-five-year-old Valentine. 'A cloud of milk', is her answer to his outburst. The 'cloud of milk', symbolically speaking, underscores the purity of her feelings – pristine whiteness covering the darkened, insalubrious realm represented by tea, which is perhaps the forbidding domain of instinct. Responding to the unvitiated nature of her feelings, Paul's emotions cascade forth like so many hollow and lifeless vestiges of a once-great literary past: his tirades are blendings of Romantic, Symbolistic, and Parnassian sentiments. The banality of his similes and personifications, and his juxtaposition of unrelated words, replicate the hypocrisy of the feelings involved. One may be outwardly lulled into believing that Paul is in love with Valentine; in reality, however, he is merely enunciating commonplaces that people repeat *ad infinitum* in theatre and in real life.

Valentine urges Paul to speak out and to liberate his feelings. Their love would then be allowed to blossom regardless of what people might say. Fear, however, enters her tangled emotions. Paul may forget her in time; more likely, she may forget him. Will he resort to the nostalgic evocation of past moments in order to keep her interested? This is an allusion perhaps to Proust's emphasis on voluntary and involuntary recall; and Freud's experiments in enticing his patients into a regressive past where they *could* be cradled, lulled into reliving infantile conditions and thereby enabled to restructure their lives.

We learn that Valentine's and François' marriage is dull and conventional. He does have 'the patience of an angel', but he acts 'like a typical businessman'. Valentine, however, is just as prosaic and dull, her world revolving around shopping trips to the department stores. Paul, who frequently accompanies her on these occasions, discusses with pleasure the oft-repeated phrase of the elevator operator: 'Going up, sir, if you please?', the statement which gives the play its title and so-called justification. In reality, however, there is no apparent link between this announcement and the rest of the proceedings, permitting the Surrealists once again to mock the artifices implicit in classical theatre: its intent to connect every facet of the play so that it forms a cohesive whole.

François enters. He is going to Geneva for a while and wants to say goodbye. He is sorry his wife won't join him. Before leaving, he in an obviously ironic statement, expresses his joy at the thought that Paul will be around to take good care of Valentine during his absence. In good old-fashioned boulevard style, he stops in front of her and then waxes lyrical: he tells her that he'll be far from her tomorrow, then he evokes the magic of new climes, the beauty of nature, devices used by the authors to emphasise the banality of romantic visions – as Flaubert accomplished so superbly, though differently, in *Madame Bovary*.

'A door closes and our life begins,' Paul states. Valentine, however, sees through him. She recognises that voice which she maintains is as false as a 'cloud', repeating the cloud image spoken at the outset of the drama. She accuses Paul of hypocrisy, of facile use of verbal bait to attract her and other women. She closes her eyes and asks him point-blank what his intentions are. In a perfectly matter-of-fact manner, he puts down his cigarette in the ash tray, takes a revolver from his pocket, aims, and Valentine slumps to the floor. The doorbell rings. Paul puts his revolver back into his pocket, relights his cigarette with great calm, and the curtain comes down.[5]

Act II has nothing to do with Act I. It takes place in an office at four o'clock in the afternoon. Létoile, played by Breton, is a forty-year-old man who sports in his lapel a rosette of the Legion of Honour. People rush in and out of his office as he dictates to his pretty young typist. The spectators know virtually nothing about Létoile's activities and hence have a sense of bewilderment, since every person *must* have a function in accordance with the running of the social structure.

Lefèvre, one of Létoile's employees, enters and proceeds to tell his boss of the important activities of the day: he saw some people who started up two side-tracked locomotives which finally overturned, and had this not happened, they would most certainly have run through two houses, underscoring the political and social ramifications of such a statement. Lefèvre leaves as another man enters. He informs Létoile that his wife's jewels have been stolen. He is urged to consult the police. Two ladies come on stage. The Second Lady begins a long speech about the poor and the suffering on this earth: the 'haggard' and the 'tattered'. When Létoile asks her how much she wants, she tells him that his heart must dictate the amount. He takes out a banknote from his wallet and gives it to her. Létoile rings for the office boy and orders him to get hold of two policemen immediately. They will explain themselves at the station house, he tells the ladies. They protest; they are not thieves, but 'licensed by the Municipal Authorities', adding irony upon irony to the scene. If this is the case, he continues, they will return the 500 francs. They do just that and Létoile proceeds to crumple the bill up, then throws it into the fire. Other humorous and satiric incidents follow.

Act III takes place in a cafe. Two men are playing cards. A woman is seated at a table: Gilda, the whore, reminiscent in name only of the beautiful, innocent, and romantic heroine of Verdi's *Rigoletto* and of Hugo's *The King Amuses Himself*. Maxime, a thirty-year-old blond man with a Van Dyck beard, sits down near Gilda. He wants to write, but is visibly disturbed. She begins reminiscing about her boarding school days, prior to her sexual education. She describes the lace collars she used to wear and the illusions she nourished about the man of her dreams. Maxime, obsessed with his own problems, speaks to her in sequences of unrelated statements. Such a dialogue, referred to medically as the Gasner Syndrome, emphasises the complete lack of relatedness between the two people. 'Soon it will be night. There will be only windmills', Gilda says. Maxime's reply, 'You can take it or leave it. Inward elegance and the craziest of desperate acts.' We learn, reading between the lines, that Gilda and Maxime are passionately in love. In time, and after a few more episodes, Maxime asks Gilda for her address so he can follow her home. She refuses to give it to him. Besides, she has syphilis, she informs him, whereupon he replies with abandon, 'Who cares?' as though it were not an uncommon condition.

After the disquietude of Act III, a long intermission is called for. Seated once again, the audience learns that the authors of *If You Please*, do not want the text of the fourth act to be enacted. Spectators are put in a state of uncertainty, what will be the conclusion of the play?

The theatre is plunged into semi-darkness. Two characters are now visible in a doorway. X looks at his watch and informs the other man of his imminent departure. Y walks up and down, speechless. We hear an irate spectator questioning: 'Is that all?'[6] In reality, an actor planted in the orchestra is voicing his displeasure with the meaningless activities on stage. 'Will you soon be finished?' he inquires. A Second Spectator voices his opinion: 'I don't understand a thing. It's idiotic.' From the box we hear a voice asking him to be silent or to leave. No, he insists, he paid for his seat and he'll stay. Another voice intervenes from the orchestra, 'If only it were interesting.' Finally, the member of the audience who first questioned the Second Spectator's right to speak now asks that he be thrown out. The fourth act is ready to begin. But the Second Spectator has grown angry and shakes his fist at the stage. Amid the tumult caused by his obstreperous behaviour one hears *'Vive la France'*, then 'Continue'. Finally the call for 'Author' is heard, and instead of Breton and Soupault walking out onstage two other actors take their place.[6]

If You Please is fascinating: in its disregard for traditional theatre, in its imaginative forays into subliminal spheres, and especially in the humour emerging from its platitudes and *non-sequiturs*. That the sets and decors are conventional is really a way of deceiving the spectators, tricking them into believing they are going to see real and understandable theatre – a boulevard play. Only as the scenes are enacted, one detached from the other, with no obvious link or meaning, do questions arise; a sense of disorientation emerges and a certain amount of malaise takes over.

3
Roger Vitrac
(1899–1952)

Victor, or The Children Take Charge (*Victor, ou Les Enfants au Pouvoir*, 1928), a three-act 'bourgeois drama' by Roger Vitrac, aims its slings and arrows at the staid middle class: those people who never sound out the possible consequences of their acts, who do not probe into their 'sacrosanct' lives; their narcissistic, materialistic, egotistical ways. Adultery, incest, scatology, patriotism, insanity, death, religion, and poetic prowess are all themes for the playwright's acid pen, to be whipped into dramatic form.

Although *Victor* is an example of Surrealist theatre it is also, to a certain degree, conventional. It has a plot to be unravelled, which many may consider absurd; there are relationships between people and families, also incredible; entrances and exits are structured within the framework of the play, but these are relatively incoherent. Although causal links in tirades or shorter speeches may be said to be neglected here and there or even willfully omitted, when they are used they encourage comparisons to be made between the protagonists' ideas, situations, and conditions. Unlike the characters of conventional theatre, however, Vitrac's creatures are wooden, marionette-like; they feel nothing as they thrash or stalk about, or walk on all fours, or slap and kick each other. In this regard they are collective figures, archetypal in dimension, and therefore important to observe and experience. Vitrac's personal brand of humour, uninhibited and even vitriolic at times, treats life and death, insanity and well-being, illness and strength with irreverence, as each performer verbally flagellates the other – all of them misfits – who mirror the society which gave birth to them.

In 1911 Vitrac and his family moved to Paris from Pinsac, in the Dordogne region of France. He completed his studies at the Collège de Chaptal, then at the Sorbonne. Although his literary idol at this period was the symbolist poet Henri de Regnier, Vitrac also revealed a genuine talent for Dada humour and its anti-logical, anti-Cartesian concatenations. He delighted his friends with his sharp wit and vitriolic banter, his finely tuned turns of phrase. After the demise of Dada, when Breton rallied around him all those who scoffed at the aesthetic and social conditions prevailing in Europe, Vitrac joined the Surrealist cause.

In 1924 Vitrac met a fellow surrealist, Antonin Artaud. They discovered they had much in common: a belief in the intrinsic freedom of the artist in all domains; a feeling for the occult and illogical side of the mind; an obsession with the notion of death and with the interplay of the body/soul dichotomy; and a metaphysical anguish. Vitrac and Artaud spent long hours discussing their future writing plans, and after their expulsion from the surrealist group they founded, together with Robert Aron, the Alfred Jarry Theatre.

The Alfred Jarry Theatre (1926)

Though the Alfred Jarry Theatre was an original theatrical enterprise, it stands to reason that the ideas and method of the man after whom it was named would come into sharp focus. Artaud and Vitrac were drawn to Jarry's literary work because of its spontaneous irrationality, its satiric and grotesque qualities, and its mystical aspects. Jarry's approach to people and things was uninhibited, his humour biting; and because he rebelled against what he considered to be the stupidity, cowardliness, greed, and hypocrisy of his age, he was thought of by many as 'eccentric'.[1]

Artaud, who drew up the manifestos outlining the general thrust of the Alfred Jarry Theatre, blended Jarry's effulgence of spirit, brutality, and irrationality with his and Vitrac's notions and emerged with a strikingly different brew from what was offered by their contemporaries.

> The spectator who comes to us knows that he has agreed to undergo a true operation, where not only his mind, but his senses and his flesh are going to come into play. Henceforth, he will go to the theatre as he does to the dentist. In the same spirit with the thought that he will not die from the ordeal, but that it is something serious and from which he will not emerge intact. If we were not convinced of being able to strike him in the most serious manner possible, we would consider ourselves incapable of carrying out our most absolute task. He must really be convinced that we are capable of making him scream out.[2]

Militantly anti-rational and hugely emotional, the Alfred Jarry Theatre would attempt to injure and spew forth venom upon all those with whom it came into contact. The aim was to divest the theatre of *all* logic and verisimilitude, and to touch and bruise the spectator, thereby forcing involvement. Only through the irrational, evocative happenings, reasoned the manifesto, could the proper atmosphere be created – where life could be pared to its essentials and so be illuminated – enabling 'reality' to emerge.

Theatre, therefore, cannot be considered as mere entertainment, nor as a gamelike activity. Rather, it is a reality, as 'unique' and unpredictable as life, and each production is 'a kind of event', a totally unexpected event. The audience becomes an intrinsic part of the theatrical venture. The spectator must be shocked, must react violently to the 'unprecedented eruption of a world' on the stage; he must feel that he is seeing the essence of his own being before him, that his life is unfolding within the bodies of others. If a theatrical production is to be considered effective, the spectator must experience anguish, be immensely and intensely involved; so deeply affected, in fact, that his whole organism is shaken into participation.[3]

The first production of the théâtre Alfred Jarry took place on 1 June 1927. It included Artaud's one-act play *Burned Stomach* or *The Mad Mother*, a lyrical 'sketch' with a musical score by Max Jacob 'which denounced humouristically the conflict between the movies and the theatre'; Roger Vitrac's *The Mysteries of Love*, a surrealistic drama which dealt with the anguish, loneliness, and sensual desire of two lovers; and *Gigogne*, a one-acter credited to Max Robur but in fact written by Robert Aron 'with the systematic aim to provoke'.[4]

The gamut of audience reaction to the inaugural performances ranged from shocked distaste to admiration – but despite Artaud's efforts, and those of the troupe as a whole, only very few responses fell into the second category. Vitrac's *Victor*, which opened on 24 December 1928, at the Comédie des Champs-Elysées, fared no better, although it was later to have a resounding reprieve.

'Victor' (1928)

Victor takes place in the apartment of the Paumelle family in Paris, on 12 September 1909. Unsparing in his details concerning the life-style of his protagonists, Vitrac lends credibility to what are extravagantly preposterous stage happenings by adhering to the classical unities of French theatre: time, action, and place. Stage time, for example, is the same as playing time: the action begins at 8.00 p.m. and continues until midnight. The Paumelle home is the seat of the antics, which revolve around two families: Emilie and Charles Paumelle, and their son, Victor; Antoine and Thérèse Magneau, and their daughter, Esther.

Act I, which opens on the Paumelles' dining room, features an enormous cake that covers virtually the entire table. On it are extremely long candles, more like tapers. Everything is so out of proportion and in such bad taste that moments after the curtains part, the audience is laughing. The lighting in this nouveau-riche milieu is as brazen as the sets: extremely bright or shadowy, the duality revealing those hidden and insalubrious recesses of the soul which people prefer to hide. The downstage suspension of empty picture frames from the ceiling was an attempt on Artaud's part to re-create the famous 'peep-hole', or fourth wall, technique of the Naturalists, inviting audiences to become voyeurs and to eavesdrop on the conversations going on behind the scenes within the tightly knit family cell.[5]

As the curtains part, the nine-year-old, six-foot Victor,

dressed in a sailor suit, is talking to the maid Lili, 'Blessed be the fruit of your gash.' Lili corrects him, 'Blessed be the fruit of your womb.' By substituting the French word *entailles* instead of using *entrailles* as called for in the Biblical text, Vitrac has ridiculed the entire religious community. Such astute manipulation of consonants and, as we will see later on, of words, clauses, and entire sentences, placed in the mouth of a child, indicates that he is genius material. Years later Vitrac referred to *Victor* as the dramatisation of the 'myth of precocious childhood', alluding to the fact that his protagonist might have been suffering from a disease called *progeria*: premature old age.

We learn that Victor's parents are going to celebrate their son's birthday that very day. They are proud of having such a brilliant offspring and must have boasted about his intellectual acumen, since Victor repeats the fact that he is 'terribly intelligent', that he has been a 'model child' until now, giving his parents complete satisfaction in everything. In fact, he has never even goosed a girl or 'pissed while shielding his eyes from the sun'.

Victor not only knows more than any adult (and tells Lily so in no uncertain terms), but is honest and perfectly frank, to the point of accusing her of being a whore and of sleeping with his father. She slaps him for his breach of etiquette. In a burst of rage, he takes a precious Baccarat glass from the table – for which his parents paid a small fortune, 3,000 francs – and threatens to smash it and blame her for the deed. Lily pleads with him. He puts it back on the table only to choose a Sèvres vase which cost his parents much more, 10,000 francs. Vitrac is obviously emphasising the materialism of the Paumelles; their values are always measured in terms of finances. Victor smashes the vase and tells Lily he will blame her for the breakage. She weeps. How could he have done such a thing? How could he have changed so drastically in the course of a few hours? In a series of absurd, side-splitting statements, which make us think of Ionesco's *The Bald Soprano*, Victor decides that he will no longer conform to the standards and patterns set by his parents.

The other 'adult' in Vitrac's play is the six-year-old Esther, who enters and tells of the strange goings on in her home. She was seated on her mother's lap when the doorbell rang. Her mother rose so suddenly that she fell on the floor. Who was at the door? Victor's father, Charles. Esther was sent to bed, and when she refused to go her mother threw a book at her which she began to look at. She listened to bizarre whisperings between the two. When Charles left, her mother began to cry. What does all this mean?

'Take care of your dolls,' Victor tells her. 'Lick your cats, love thy neighbour as thyself . . . until such time as you become a good wife and mother.' Then he begins to pun, rhyme, in absolutely irrational verbal arrangements, introducing the characters soon to people the stage: The *Enfant Terrible*, the Unworthy Father, the Good Mother, the Adulterous Wife, the Cuckold. The audience is now prepared to meet the Paumelles and the Magneaus. Who broke the Sèvres vase? Charles and Emilie ask. Esther, of course, Victor replies, and to prove the veracity of his statement he says: 'You see she is crying.' What better proof of her guilt is there? Circumstantial evidence is in his favour.

Moments later, Antoine, Esther's father, enters. His speech is so rapid, his ideas so incongruous, that another disruptive note is added to the scene. Antoine wishes Victor a happy birthday, utters the usual platitudes as he tells him he is growing taller every day, and asks him his age without bothering to listen for an answer. His family thinks he is crazy. Antoine is a man who lives on his war memories – those good old days when heroes stalked the earth – and he relates everything he says to a 'fabulous' past, to the military deeds connected with the Franco-Prussian War. As his vision of times gone by grows more acute, he begins hearing guns and canons as if he were on a battlefield; the rhythm of his soliloquy speeds up and his voice grows louder and louder. 'Long Live the First Consul!' he shouts as he salutes, sings, then recites the facts surrounding the life of Achille Bazaine, Marshal of France, who distinguished himself in the Crimean and Mexican wars but betrayed his country during the Franco-Prussian War.

To enhance the confusion and antagonism – as well as the playful atmosphere of this work – General Etienne Lonségur makes his appearance. Commenting on Victor's height and wisdom, the general suggests that he will make a good soldier when he grows up. Victor, whose insight and precocity are unparalleled and whose sadistic bent is equally well developed, intends again to bring up the subject of Bazaine, thereby arousing Antoine to a state of hysteria and causing Thérèse no end of embarassment.

The lights dim; the guests take their seats at the table. Victor is asked to make a toast. Since 'it's for France,' he agrees and begins singing a war song. Antoine is again aroused and relives the great and tragic incidents during France's hour of defeat at Sedan; her spoliation, disgrace. 'Pigs, pigs,' he calls out compulsively, brashly. To increase the insanity of the stage antics, three separate conversations are enacted virtually simultaneously: a technique used by the Surrealists to ward off any possible logical reaction on the part of the audience. Victor and Emilie, the two adults, are playing at being parents; the others are embedded in their adulterous imbroglios, egotism, and war games. The accentuating and slackening of the vocal rhythms, the atonal and detached manner in which the protagonists articulate their speeches, are uproariously farcical, but the callousness of their attitudes, their marionette-like mannerisms and relationships, are symptomatic of beings divested of all feeling. When the general gets down on all fours and plays horsee, whinnying, kicking, and rearing, with Victor holding on as he rides him – a degrading posture for such a pillar of society – anything is possible. To make the situation even more realistic, Victor gives his horse a piece of sugar, then orders him to trot and gallop, while Esther is doubled over with laughter as she watches his madcap play.

Act II takes place in the Paumelles' living room. A three-foot tall palm tree stands at the centre of the stage. The guilty couple are afraid that their affair, which was merely alluded to in Act I, may now be common knowledge. Do Victor and Esther suspect something? Thérèse grows increasingly tense. Charles reassures her; then begins caressing her, drags her to the divan, pushes her onto it. 'It's too late,' Thérèse protests. 'It's too late,' Victor repeats, having hidden behind a piece of furniture so as to better observe the 'adults' in this compromising position.

Victor is told to go to bed. 'With whom?' the lad asks. 'With whom?' repeats Charles, exasperated. 'With whom? I don't know; with Esther, with your mother, if you want.' Freudian innuendos of incest are apparent as Victor proceeds to demolish everything that is considered sacred in society. Angered to the point of distraction, Charles takes a vase and smashes it; then he begins dancing a jig. 'To live a whole evening like this,' he states, 'is impossible. We need a miracle.' No sooner said than – and perhaps this is the climax of this hallucinatory sequence – a strikingly beautiful woman in evening dress, bedecked with jewels and furs, and coiffed with egrets, makes her entrance. 'The miracle!' Victor shouts.

Ida Mortemart, the strange woman in question, is one of the most extraordinary and ingeniously constructed characters in French theatre. For Artaud, who wrote at length about her, she 'concretised' anguish; she was the catalyst who paved the way for the increasingly paroxysmal behaviour of the characters in this 'willfully truthful' play, with its 'cruel light which glares down on the lowest and dirtiest depths of the human unconscious'. Along with the 'incontestable perversity' of the play, is its 'magic,' its 'reality', at times acute and oblique, which is brought into sharp relief by Ida Mortemart and her terrible weakness – a weakness that 'underscores the profound and eternal antithesis between the enslavement to our material state and functions, and our qualities as angels and pure spirits.'[6]

Ida Mortemart is death incarnate: a great presence, majestic in her stance, her measured gestures, the coldness and reserve of her facial expressions, the pallor of her skin. When she enters, she brings suggestions of shock and terror with her. She questions Emilie. Does Emilie recognise her? No, Emilie answers at the outset of a hilarious sequence which turns on an irrational interplay of statements. It seems they knew each other years back. Or did they? They agree that they both lived on the same street when they were children. Perhaps they never met. It's all so strange! In supercilious tones, Charles, speaking for Vitrac, adds a final flourish to the interchange when he says to Ida, 'Well madame, if a dramatist had used this stratagem to make you appear here, and at this very moment, we would have screamed out unbelievable!' But it is 'the simple truth,' Ida reiterates.

The general chimes in and reverts to what he knows best, his military occupation. Farcically he states, 'Imagine, madame, if they asked for a canon.' 'A canon!' the lady retorts, visibly upset. Then she farts. Esther is beside herself with laughter, but Victor, painfully embarrassed, does not budge. 'It's incredible. It must be a joke,' the general suggests. Ida is mortified and confesses, 'I can't, I can't' whereupon she farts again. She cannot control herself. She suffers from a terrible sickness. Another fart. This time it's a long one. Whenever she is emotionally disturbed, she says, she loses control and her infirmity takes over. She again farts. Gradually the laughter abates, as do the well-time crescendos and diminuendos of the musical accompaniment.

In frank and sober terms, but wearing an expression of controlled melancholy, she tells of her wealth, her many homes, automobiles, diamonds, children, her husband, the banker. After more sonorous emanations, she finally invites Victor and Esther to sit on her lap. Terrified by this phantom-like apparition, Esther runs out of the house. Her fear of the strange woman is understandable, as the first syllable of her name, *mort*, means death in French. When she enters a home, she is that force which cuts down life, announces heartbreak. Esther, being a child, lives closer to nature than an adult, and she senses a condition that the older people overlook. Esther does not want to die. Victor, suffering from progeria, has already lived out his earthly span, his time is up. But before he dies Victor tells Ida, when they are alone, that he would like to know something about making love. She can't tell him, she answers; she's too embarrassed. He insists, whereupon she whispers something in his ear and leaves. It is then that his face wears an appearance of unmitigated sadness.

Act III is reminiscent, in its comic aspects, of a Feydeau bedroom farce, and it is indeed enacted in the Paumelles' bedroom, but it is a farce clouded with tragedy. As it begins, Charles is reminiscing about the day's events, punning on Ida Mortemart's name. He walks, dances, prances about, then bends down to kiss his wife. She protests. 'Not tonight'. Then he won't go to bed, he tells her. He'll finish his carpentry. He takes out nails, hammer, and saw and begins planing the wooden bed frame. 'He's crazy! Completely mad!' Emilie cries out, after which she throws herself on the bed sobbing. He pursues his work oblivious to her feelings. The rhythm of his hammering and nailing slackens, as if a slow motion film were being shown; while he works he recites humorous, off-colour ditties. Suddenly, to add to the absurdity of the scene, Emilie jumps on her husband's back and he throws her off with a simple shrug of the shoulders. She falls on the floor, picks up a hammer, and mounts him again, this time with hand raised, intending, perhaps, to do the worst. But Charles pacifies her, takes the hammer away from her, and carries her to the bed. The lights dim. They are off to sleep. But Charles can't rest. He gets up, talks to himself, and gets so worked up that he begins hurling syllables here and there in loud metallic tones. Emilie, besides herself with grief and rage, screams out a prayer to the Virgin Mary, 'I salute you Mary, full of grace The Lord with you. . .'

The scene with its carefully orchestrated shouts and sighs, its rapid and slack rhythms, its humour and pathos, runs the gamut of theatrical styles. It is farce at its best, spreading shock, bewilderment, and comprehension. Dancing, parading, falling, tumbling – in short, the ridiculous – allied to the satirical, the poignant, and even the tragic, which makes painful inroads – gashes – into the protagonists' inner worlds. When, at the outset of the play, Victor said 'Blessed be the fruit of your gash', he was forewarning audiences of the situation, the complexity of the antithetical feelings and ideas existing in the family cell:

husband and wife, children and parents, each hurting, branding, cutting the other, creating that bleeding gash which can never be healed.

Victor enters. He tells his parents they are making so much noise he can't sleep. Besides, he's sick. Charles does not believe him and tells him he should go to the bathroom, take some water, breathe in and out – exactly what parents tell their children when they want to get rid of them. He is afraid his parents are going to kill each other. He knows his father keeps a revolver next to the potty. He leaves.

More incredible antics. The lights go out. Victor is heard crying and groaning. Charles, in bed with his wife, hears none of it. He speaks to her serenely. The contrapuntal effects of the sighs and moans outside the room and the harmonious murmurs within create tension and work on the spectators' nerves. Charles tells his wife of his love for Thérèse, including in his speech all the erotic details and images he can think of. Emilie is not jealous. Suddenly, prolonged and agonising screams are heard. The parents pay no heed. They pursue their conversation and passionate epithets, intermixed with neologisms, puns, and word associations in this comedy of errors. Thérèse enters. She's in a panic. Where is Esther? She has disappeared. Surely she must be with Victor, since she wanted him to be her little father. The Freudian incestuous intent in this statement is obvious. No sooner do Emilie and Charles tell her that Esther is not in their home than she appears at the door.

The surreal world has taken over completely as Emilie, now in a state of religious ecstasy, begins praying, fervently passionately, thanking God and Heaven for having sent Esther to them. Emilie orders everyone to get down on their knees with her and pray, and so they do: the adulterous wife, the unworthy father, the unfortunate mother, and the children all make confession. They will renounce their evil ways.

Moments later we learn that Antoine has hanged himself and Victor has fainted from pain. Emilie carries him on stage and speaks to him endearingly in mock baby language. Victor moves ever so slightly. He's not dead, she says. But then why doesn't he answer? He's persecuting his parents, she decides, and with that she slaps her son. To brutalise a dying child, Victor says, coming to for a moment, instills guilt into a heartless and brainless mother who does not know any other way to act. Victor informs her about the fate of other precocious children: Hercules and the serpents who tried to strangle him in his crib; and Mozart and Jesus, proclaimed the Son of God when he was born. To be compared to them adds yet another burden to the already most *intelligent* of children. He has to die, he informs his parents – and on his ninth birthday. So it is proclaimed.[7]

After the doctor arrives and takes Victor's temperature rectally, he gives his prognosis, 'He is dying of . . .' Victor interrupts, 'I am dying of Death.' The doctor leaves. A black curtain falls onto the stage. Two shots are heard. The curtain rises. Emilie and Charles are lying at the foot of Victor's bed, separated by a still-smoking revolver. The maid appears. 'But its a drama!' she exclaims, a statement which may sum up the theatrical experience in a variety of ways: drama, implying excitement, suspense, and pain; also associated with Denis Diderot's concept of drama as representation of problems wracking the middle class in the eighteenth century – and by extension in the twentieth, all society.

Victor, which ridicules every aspect of human behaviour and accomplishment and demolishes in shocking, abrasive sequences, whatever illusions one may have harboured concerning people and society, was received coldly in 1928. Referred to as a 'poetic parody,' it is a play consisting of fragmentary visions and divided sequences, and it left audiences and critics alike questioning, dissatisfied, frustrated – and bored. They did not really know how to react to what purported to be their moral and physical ugliness. People were perhaps not yet ready to question their motivations and relationships.

On 12 November 1946, Michel de Ré, a young director, produced *Victor*, with his Compagnie du Thyase and included music by Henri Sauguet. Even after World War II, even when psychoanalysis had gained ground and hypocrisies had been besmirched, characters debased, Victor was not a commercial success. Critics were supercilious, writing of *Victor*'s farcical side, its artificiality, its arbitrariness, the absurdity of its plot, the bad taste of its humour. A 'real stew,' one commentator called it; it seemed to have few redeeming features. Furthermore, critics contended that Surrealism was no longer revolutionary; it had passed its prime so that problems dramatised in *Victor* were no longer applicable. The avant-garde has become rear guard. Nevertheless, the company as a whole was lauded for its verve and dynamism, its fine acting and the scope of the direction.[8]

When *Victor* was again produced in 1962 at the Ambigu Theatre in Paris, and the director was Jean Anouilh, the play won a resounding success. As director, Anouilh allied Feydeau-like elements – that is, comic and absurd effects coupled with a vaudeville atmosphere – with Strindbergian tragedy in what was alluded to as a 'cynical ballet-like' theatrical event. What many could not understand is why Anouilh, who always kept in the background and who rarely allowed himself to be interviewed, chose to create the mise-en-scene for *Victor*. 'I am trying to rectify an injustice', he told a reporter. He owed much to Vitrac, who had encouraged him to write years back. They had remained in contact during all that time. When Anouilh saw *Victor* in 1946, the play so inspired him that he incorporated certain themes in his own work *Ardèle*. Then Anouilh had second thoughts. He asked Vitrac whether he should change his script because it was so close to *Victor*. Vitrac told him to leave it as is.[9]

With Anouilh's stamp of approval, *Victor* – and this comes as no surprise – was lauded by virtually every critic: for its excitement, its living qualities, its insolence, its linguistic gymnastics, its incongruity, its provocative and mysterious nature, its humour, its acerbity – those very characteristics that had been deplored in 1928 and overlooked in 1946. Artaud's premonitory statement concerning *Victor* was: 'You ask me what I expect from this daring and scandalous play: it's very simple. I expect everything.'[10] And indeed it has everything.

4
Antonin Artaud
(1896–1948)

Artaud had opted for a theatre that worked on the nerves and senses, and rejected one which sought to speak to the intellect alone. His Theatre of Cruelty, as described in his essays and manifestos (1931–35) published in *The Theatre and its Double* (1938), derides everything that is logical and suggests a search be made to seek out the 'marvellous', the hidden and mysterious forces within humankind and nature. 'Beware of your logic, Sirs, beware of your logic,' he wrote, 'you don't know to what lengths our hatred for the logical can lead us.'[1] Artaud's attacks on reason in the arts, on education, and on conventional modes of thinking in general reflected perfectly his own mental deficiencies and explain in part his affinity with the Surrealists. What was faulty within Artaud's psychological makeup was his inability to think in a Cartesian manner. Hence his rejection of the status quo *en bloc*. For him, more than for the Surrealists, his attitude disclosed an unconscious desire to banish everything that smacked of normality. With the reign of the illogical, Artaud would be one of many, like the others; no longer a recluse, tormented by the vast gulf that separated him from society.

Artaud was born in Marseilles. At the age of five he suffered almost unbearable head pains which developed into meningitis. He was cured of this almost always fatal sickness, but the aftereffects were to last him for the rest of his life. In 1914, when he was about to take his baccalaureate examination, for no apparent reason he became despondent. He then suffered an episode of neurasthenia and was sent to a rest home. Some months later his health improved and he was returned to his family. In 1916 he was drafted into the infantry, but nine months later he had become so mentally unstable that he was released and went home. He was sent to another rest home in Switzerland, where he remained for two years. His condition improved, and he was sent to Paris so that he could nurture his artistic bent.

In Paris in 1920, Artaud began writing and acting. He performed in Lugné-Poë's company, in Charles Dullin's and with Georges Pitoëff. It soon became obvious to Artaud and to his employers, that his inner turmoil and his overly personal, too-intense approach to roles made it difficult, if not impossible, to work with him and still maintain troupe discipline and harmony.

Artaud had sufficient insight into himself and others to realise that the performing phase of his theatrical career was passing. He would have to find a different way to express himself. Imprisoned as he was in his subjective anguish, his life was made endurable only by a fascination with his inner world, which stirred and captivated his imagination. It is understandable, then, that he should have joined the Surrealists (1924), for they, too, wanted to expand humankind's concept of reality and give credence to the unconscious as a liberating force, freeing people from the grasping tentacles of an overly constricting moralistic bourgeois society and its literary and artistic convention. He was summarily ejected from the fold by Breton in 1926, the same year which marked the founding of the Alfred Jarry Theatre.

The Theatre and its Double: The Theatre of Cruelty

In 1922 Artaud attended the Colonial Exhibition in Marseilles, where he watched the sacred Cambodian dancers perform before a reproduction of the Temple of Angkor Wat. Nine years later, he witnessed a production of the Balinese Theatre at the Colonial Exhibition in Paris. Both times he was impressed by the spectacle: by the metaphysical terror he experienced when seeing strange and horrifying forms – dragons and other inhuman mani-festations – appearing onstage before him. Dread had been aroused, he now realised, by something *concrete* and not by language, an abstraction. Inhuman and divine forms suddenly stalked the stage – manifestations of a world beyond the known. Oriental theatre, then, was not psychologically oriented; a production was looked upon as a sacred ceremony, where spectators could undergo a metaphysical experience. As for the text of the play performed, it was merely a 'poetic framework' from which the rest of the production emanated.

What also fascinated Artaud was the importance accorded to gesture and facial expression in Balinese and Cambodian theatrical performances, and the relatively unimportant role delegated to the spoken word. The visible action onstage had its impact upon a person's unconscious. Gesture became a transforming agent, communicating to the spectators mysterious and hitherto unrevealed contents stemming from the author's, the director's, and the actors' unconscious and conscious worlds. An elevated arm, a lowered finger, a twist of the head, eyes focussed to the left, all had symbolic power. Considered from this point of view, gestures, as well as lighting and sound effects, Artaud suggested, are laden with magical force empowered to titillate and arouse the senses.

Artaud was convinced that words are incapable of expressing certain attitudes and feelings, and that these can be revealed only through gestures or sounds, symbolically felt. 'All true feeling is in reality untranslatable. To express it is to betray it. But to translate it is to *dissimulate it*.'[2] Therefore objects, music, chanting, costumes, gestures, *and* words, used together, are much more effective in bringing about powerful reactions in the spectator than are words used either alone or as primal factors in the spectacle. Non-verbal dramatic devices are transformed by each spectator, who interprets them symbolically into the images he feels the action demands. They take on, therefore, both personal and impersonal meaning. A ball of red cloth, 'for example, displayed in a certain way onstage, implies the cutting off of an actor's head. Imitative harmonies, such as the hissing of serpents or the buzzing of insects', Artaud wrote, 'lend a metaphysical and awesome quality to a production.' Artaud went still further. He pointed out that all the operative elements in Oriental theatre (music, costumes, objects, words, gestures, etc.) leave no space unutilised. A *concrete* sculptural quality, which fills the void about the actor, is therefore created onstage, adding to the visual enjoyment of the spectacle and at the same time capturing the theatre's essential qualities: its metaphysical and spiritual aspects.[3]

Artaud sought to create an Occidental drama that would

take on the solemn and frightening aspects of Oriental theatre and encourage the 'inner eye' to become operative. He looked upon everything onstage as symbolic, as a sign behind which lies a mysterious, fabulous, and dangerous reality. For the Westerner, reality resides in appearances, show, facade: for the Oriental and for Artaud, true reality resides in the world within, which resembles the Westerner's dream world. It was the Oriental's reality, corresponding to the Westerner's unconscious world, that Artaud wished to represent on the stage.

In addition to reflecting humanity's inner world, the theatre, because of its metaphysical and religious nature, said Artaud, must be a manifestation of cosmic reality. Consequently, author, actor, director, spectator, objects, colour, sound, gesture, movements, rhythms, and words in the theatre arena must be looked upon as differentiations or parts of the cosmic whole. Space, therefore, is seen as something alive – as part of the cosmic flow and not distinct from it.

Furthermore, since the theatre should be looked upon as a religious ritual, Artaud advocated a theatre based on myth. A myth is defined as a dramatic relating of those experiences or a description of those qualities which are deepest within humanity. Myths are the outcome of original experiences – not always personal, but sometimes impersonal or trancendental. In ancient times, for example, people believed that flowers, rocks, water, ice – all of nature's forces – were inhabited by gods. Primitive humans did not just watch the sun rise and set and accept it as such. They assimilated this external experience so that it became an inner one. For instance, they likened the story of the sun's daily journey through the skies to a hero's fate. They did likewise with everything in nature: rain, thunder, harvest, drought. The fascinating and terrifying images produced in peoples; unconscious as a result of their experiences took the form of dreams and premonitions; they became symbolic expressions of an inner drama which they could only cope with by projecting it onto nature or the environment. These projected dramas, or myths, transcended the individual conscious mind in that they occurred everywhere, to all of humankind. Every culture has its creation myth, its god myth, its hero myth, and so on, and these myths, whose origins are in many cases pre-historic, were recorded sooner or later in one form or another.[4]

That the theatre of antiquity enacted humankind's dreams and fantasies (myths) made possible the release of psychic energy in the spectator. To merely reproduce the myths of the ancients on a modern stage would be absolutely pointless to Artaud's way of thinking. New myths, therefore, must come into being, and quickly, because western people today feel cut off from nature and from themselves. Rational and scientific developments have given society a clearer understanding of its relation-ship to nature, but as a result people no longer participate in its mysteries. A cliff is a cliff, plain and simple; it is no longer a source of magic, fright, and excitement as it was for the ancients. Primitive peoples became familiar with their inner dreams through analogy with the process of nature. Today individuals must find their way alone, unaided by alliance with God, nature, or themselves. It is the task of the writer to discover his or her own sentiments about life, to dredge up from the depths the fire that lives within, to force down the mask and reveal the inner sun, though it may be coated with black.

Artaud called the theatre he wished to see come into being 'The Theatre of Cruelty'. It was a theatre which aimed to activate a person's 'magnetic' nervous system to such an extent as to enable him or her to project feelings and sensations beyond the usual limits imposed by time and space. This kind of theatre would make it possible for audiences to have a powerful metaphysical experience while watching the spectacle onstage and feel cleansed and purified, ready for rebirth, afterward.

What is 'cruelty'? As used by Artaud, it does not mean 'blood' or 'carnage,' though these might occur during a performance. The word 'cruelty' must be considered from a philosophical point of view: to create, to breathe, to cry – any act – is cruelty.

> I employ the word 'cruelty' in the sense of an appetite for life, a cosmic rigor, an implacable necessity, in the gnostic sense of a living whirlwind that devours the darkness, in the sense of that pain apart from whose ineluctable necessity life could not continue; good is desired, it is the consequences of an act; evil is permanent.[5]

Everything that is not dormant in life is cruel. When Brahma, for example, left his state of rest, he suffered. When a child is born, it knows pain. Death, transformation, fire, love, appetite, are all cruelties. The moment unity no longer exists, pain must follow. Any change in a state of being requires motion, and in that motion – a change from dark to light, matter to spirit, inertia to movement – conflict and cruelty begin. When God created the world, he did away with the original state of unity. When he cast Adam and Eve from paradise, he further increased the division between humanity and himself, and humanity and the cosmos. Before the Creation, and before Adam and Eve were cast forth into the world of antagonisms, life did not exist as we now perceive it – paradise is in actuality a state of union with the cosmos.

What Artaud called 'the Great Fable of Creation,' that is, the change from unconscious unity to conscious individuality and multiplicity, is forever being enacted on different levels, and is, Artaud felt, a human being's most traumatic experience. Drama *per se*, looked upon symbolically, is the drama of Creation. In each great theatrical work, the writer enacts and re-enacts the pain experienced when he or she was torn away from the original unity experienced with mother, or, psychologically speaking, was wrenched from an unconscious or undifferentiated reality to a state of multiplicity or consciousness, in which it was necessary to act and react, and therefore, in Artaud's words, 'live cruelly'.[6]

As the spectator sees and hears the story of creation (in one form or another) enacted before him onstage, he is filled with nostalgia for the primordial condition he once knew. To reach this deepest of levels, a march inward must be made. Such motion is shocking and painful; it is action pushed to the extreme. 'Everything that acts is a cruelty. It is upon this idea of extreme action, pushed beyond all limits, that theatre, must be rebuilt.'

The Theatre of Cruelty, as conceived by Artaud, is a total experience: material and spiritual, real and imaginary. Theatrical techniques for such a theatre must be precise, and as well organised, Artaud suggested, as the circulation of blood in the arteries. For it to be mythical and numinous, theatre must furnish real subjects that emanate from people's dreams: crime, eroticism, desire for utopia, cannibalism and incest. If the theatre, in such a case, turns out to be inhuman, then it is a reflection of a person's spasmodic and antagonistic inner life, the result of having been ejected into the world and forced to live cruelly.

The specific elements of a Theatre of Cruelty spectacle will now be taken up one by one: the role of the director; the actor and the breathing technique; gestures; words; sound effects; lighting; the stage and the theatre; objects; masks; accessories; decors; the play itself.

The director, according to Artaud, is like a magician, a master of 'sacred ceremonies', a 'Demiurge'. He is a high priest, a God, a type of 'unique creator' who brings about fusion of all the disparate theatrical elements and thereby creates unity from disunity. The director, therefore, animates the spectacle and the action – all the world which comes to life, even matter – and weaves it into a dramatic pattern which acts directly upon the spectator.

If a director's function in part is to infuse life into the spectacle, the actor must do likewise when creating a role. An actor must materialise the sensations and feelings he seeks to bring out in his portrayal and can effect such a result through proper breathing. Passion of every type has 'organic bases', Artaud wrote. It is something physical and the rays emitted by a sensation from the body are likewise material. Every mental motion, every feeling, has its corresponding breath, Artaud stated. It is the actor who must discover the right breath for the proper sentiment.

The actor, through breathing, can also create a being, that is, his double: the character he wants to personify, or an image or a mood. He can learn to commune with the forces of nature as well as with his own disparate parts by localising the points where his muscles are affected by the emotion he seeks to portray. To know the secret of breathing is to be able to provoke life, to divine the colour of the soul, which is not pure abstraction but is also made of matter, 'The soul can be physiologically reduced to a skein of vibrations'. Artaud affirmed that one can go still further, stating that through breathing one could reach a more profound reality and return to one's origins. If an actor, he explained, does not possess a certain feeling necessary for his part, he can 'sink into himself' by means of breathing and there discover and connect with the feelings he seeks to express. The theatre, looked upon in this manner, becomes 'the perfect and the most complete symbol of universal manifestation'. The actor carries within him part of the cosmos and can return into it through his own organism, through his lungs.[7]

Furthermore, the actor must know how to *touch* certain parts of the spectator's body in order to send him into a 'magnetic trance'. He can succeed in this because emotion has organic origins. When breathing properly, the actor casts forth certain rays which strike the spectator in the proper place, provoking him to laugh or cry, as the case may be. Unlike the western actor, who looks *out*, who is 'uplifted toward God' or to his role, and who 'succumbs to exaltation' when he experiences religious fervour, Artaud's actor, like the Oriental, looks *within* to find God, or his double.

Gesture is also of extreme importance in creating a momentous theatrical spectacle. It reveals the inner person. 'Gesture is [the theatre's] material and its wit; and, if you will, its alpha and omega.'[8] Gestures, however, must not be confused with pantomime, Artaud declared, for the latter is a deformation of the mute elements of Italian comedy. Gestures are symbolic evocations of nature's aspects. They are signs of both inner and outer activities which can be made onstage and which act upon the spectator's imagination.

Though gestures and attitudes on the part of the actor are of supreme importance in Artaud's theatre, words should not be 'suppressed' in creating a stage language. They should be given the importance they have in dreams,

Artaud stated. The word is but one of many theatrical vehicles – to be combined with lighting, gestures, music, sound, facial expressions and other elements. Western theatre relies too heavily upon the spoken word as a vehicle for expression. As a result, the word has become an ossified and frozen means of conveying feeling, magic, and mystery in the theatre. Artaud was intent upon restoring to the theatre that which had been dethroned by Racine and his contemporaries when they gave primacy to the word and the psychological play.

Artaud relegated the word to its proper place as one of the ways of expressing and acting upon humanity's inner world. If words are to be effective, they must be manipulated like solid objects, Artaud explicated. They must act and react upon each other and upon the spectator. The word is a concrete reality for Artaud and it must be uttered with the vehemence of the emotion that gave birth to it. Words are not merely a means of communication. Artaud sought to restore to them their primitive functions and qualities, their incantatory nature, supernatural aura, mesmerising and magical faculties, all lost to modern humanity. To re-create the role of the word necessitated first its destruction. Established words, meanings, and sounds would have to be shattered before new content could emerge. Words then would become like hieroglyphics, visual translations of certain mysterious elements within humanity and the universe.

The notations Artaud made for the sound effects to be used in his dramatic productions were so detailed that they resembled a musical score. But even these descriptions indicating the concrete sounds he sought to reproduce in the course of a play could not possibly convey the sought-for impression, since no verbal depiction of a sound or vocal intonation or nuance is really possible. Musical instruments, if needed during a theatrical performance, should also be used as objects; as in oriental plays, they should be symbolic parts of the decor. If modern instruments cannot produce the sounds the director considers necessary to his production, then ancient instruments should be used or new ones invented. (Artaud noted that special blendings of new metal alloys could add new pitches to an octave and produce unbearable noises.)

Lights should be like protagonists in the play, actors, part of the performance. The interplay of lights on the stage can be a dramatic instrumentality designed to create an atmosphere capable of moving the spectator to anxiety, terror, eroticism, or love. Lighting is a force which can play on the mind of the spectator because of its vibratory possibilities. It can, Artaud declared, be cast down onto the stage in waves, in sheets, or in fiery arrows.

Costumes can be exquisite works of art as they are in the oriental theatre; they can also capture the magic and mystery of the unknown. Modern dress, Artaud felt, should be avoided since it does not arouse the imagination. There should be no separation between the stage and the theatre. The theatre should be enclosed within four walls and be modified according to the architecture of certain sacred places: churches or temples, such as those in Tibet. There should be no ornamentation and the walls should be painted with lime to absorb the light. Audiences should sit in the middle of the stage on movable chairs, which would permit them to follow the play unfolding around them. There should be galleries in the theatre, allowing the action to take place on all levels and in all dimensions. This diffused action in space would grip and assault the spectator, as though a world were forcing itself in upon him: symbolically speaking, the outside world acting upon and stimulating a person's inner sphere.

Antonin Artaud

The sense of the fragmentary and isolated nature of life as experienced in a series of diverse visual moments was, in part, what Artaud and the Surrealists sought to express in their paintings, films, poetry, and theatre. Artaud did not believe in the necessity for a visual centre in a theatrical production. In the theatre, the audience must see a performance not as a concentrated whole, but as a succession of fragments or moments isolated in space. The rational mind must not synthesise or order the images it sees into consecutive patterns. Life itself is in a state of flux. It is the impact of isolated fragments upon the spectator that is important.

Masks and other objects were to be used in the Theatre of Cruelty to help create a concrete theatrical language. These accessories and masks could appear on stage in the same size and shape as they do in the sleeper's dream world. They could, therefore, be huge or tiny, grotesque or beautiful – infinitely varied.

There was to be no decor, Artaud wrote. It must be noted that in old Chinese theatre there was no attempt at realistic scenery. The stage was decorated – that is, it indicated where the action was situated – in a palace, on a lake, etc. – but it did not actually represent the location. Properties were used symbolically: a wooden table and two chairs might imply a banquet hall. Artaud felt that his actors, whom he called 'animated hieroglyphics,' could, by the rhythmic use of their voices and their gestures, express everything that was necessary.

A play must be topical, Artaud wrote, modern in its specifics and corresponding to humanity's present problems and preoccupations. Its general themes, however, should be universal and myth-like, revealing the totality of humankind: social upheavals, conflicts of peoples, races, natural forces.

75

Artaud's theatre (his plays, *Jet of Blood* [*Le Jet de Sang*], 1925; *The Cenci*, 1935; his philosophical work, *The Theatre and its Double*) was designed to reflect cosmic reality, to inflict cruelty, that is, to be a theatre of 'extreme action, pushed beyond all limits', bombarding each and every spectator from all parts of the theatre with sensations of all kinds; transforming the amorphous into the plastic, thereby creating a concrete poetry in space.

The Jet of Blood not only stands as a landmark in Artaud's development, but also as a bizarre and highly original anti-theatrical brew which has gone a long way in influencing the theatre of the absurd as well as other contemporary so-called classical dramas. Although Artaud had announced its production in the literature he published in connection with the Alfred Jarry Theatre, *The Jet of Blood* was not staged until 1964. At this time Peter Brook and Charles Marowitz performed it in their Theatre of Cruelty programme at the *Lamda* Theatre in London.

In *The Jet of Blood*, Artaud attacks the political, social, and religious attitudes of the day in frequently stock and hackneyed epithets and phrases. Derisive and macabre humour, suffused with a sense of dread and despair, creates, strangely enough, sequences that are deliriously funny as well as terrifying. Far more than a criticism of society, *The Jet of Blood* is a revelation of Artaud's own inner life: his difficulties in adjusting to manhood and his struggle to make some connection between inner and outer reality. What Artaud sets before his viewers, however, is anything but personal. It is, on the contrary, an anonymous collective world, detached and objective. Even the cast is impersonal, each character appearing as a function rather than an individual with a name: the Young Man, the Young Girl, the Wet Nurse, etc.

The play opens as a young boy and girl say to each other,

'I love you and everything is beautiful'. This statement is repeated by both boy and girl with variations in tonal and rhythmical values, like a litany or joyful refrain, expressing the intensity of their emotions, the boy and girl represent youth and idealism, satisfaction with the *status quo*, the state of childhood contentment, reminiscent of Adam and Eve in paradise. Suddenly, there is silence. One hears the noise of an immense wheel turning, and a feeling of terror is aroused as a storm breaks. During the course of the storm stars collide: legs, hands, columns, masks, and other items fall from heaven in slow motion as if into a void.

The world is no longer beautiful now that the Young Man and the Young Girl have fallen onto earth, or matter. It has become ugly, sordid, and dangerous. The Young Man looks up toward heaven, 'The sky has gone mad!' The differentiated world of the adult can now be seen, divided and disoriented. The triunal aspect of the cosmos also comes into view as a scorpion crawls upon the earth, ejecting its poison at will; as a frog, living on land and in water, hops into view; and as a scarab, worshipped as a spirit by the Egyptians, takes on form. These represent three facets of existence: the will of the conscious mind, the amorphous material of the unconscious sphere, and the spiritual character of the upper regions. Aspects that were once unified in the innocence of childhood are now, in adulthood, divided and in conflict with each other, arousing hatred, lust, fanaticism – and disgust.

The Young Man and the Young Girl flee in fear from this new world. A Knight in shining armour appears onstage with his heavy-breasted Wet Nurse. The Knight seems to symbolise past strength and grandeur, but the audience is in for a surprise: instead of being a sturdy and courageous knight of old, he turns out to be an emotional weakling. He asks his Wet Nurse for the Gruyère cheese she is carrying

77

wrapped in paper, implying that this adult-boy is still in need of the nourishing (cheese) principle of his Wet Nurse-Mother. She, on the other hand, tries to distract him by pointing to the Young Man and the Young Girl, who are making love. The Knight could not care less.

The Young Man now appears on the scene, declaring, 'I have seen, I have learned, I have understood.' Then society's representatives come forward: a priest, a shoemaker, a procuress, a judge, and others. The priest puts his arm around the Young Man's neck, and in confessional tones wonders which part of the girl's body the Young Man will allude to most frequently. Hoping for some kind of lewd answer, he is annoyed when the Young Man speaks in sincere and innocent terms and names God.

Darkness suddenly engulfs everything; there are great peals of thunder and flashes of lightning and then an enormous hand comes down and seizes the procuress by the hair. But she bites the hand of God and blood spurts from his wrist. Having *experienced* pain and anguish, she acts out her aggressions and blasphemes. Having overthrown old concepts and fables, she and the Young Man rush into each other's arms. At this moment the Wet Nurse returns, carrying the Young Girl, who is now dead. When the Knight sees his Wet Nurse, he shakes her; he wants more Gruyère. The ambivalence of their relationship is made more obvious when she raises her skirts. As he curses his Wet Nurse, scorpions emerge from beneath her skirt and 'begin to swarm into her sex,' which Artaud writes 'swells and splits,' becoming vitreous, and even glittering like a sun. Clearly an allusion to the Book of Revelation (ch. 9: 1–3), it is not only a premonitory image of the destruction of the world but also an image of Artaud's own fear and rejection of the Earth-Woman in all her avatars. That the Young Man and the Procuress now flee, then, is expected. As for the Young Girl, she arises almost as in a miracle play, and, dazzled, says, 'The Virgin! Ah! That's what he was searching for, the primordial image of the woman in all her pristine purity, as in the figure of the Virgin Mary: heaven-sent, heaven-inseminated, and not of this world.'

Artaud's *The Cenci* which opened at the Folies-Wagram theatre in Paris on 6 May, 1935, was based on his version of Shelley's five-act tragedy (1819) by the same name and on Stendhal's translation (1837) of a sixteenth-century account of an historical event. The facts are uncomplicated. Beatrice Cenci was the daughter of Francesco Cenci (1549–1598), a sordid, cruel, sexually perverted Roman nobleman. His first wife had died after bearing him seven children. He then married the wealthy and beautiful Lucretia Petroni. Later, he plotted the death of his sons and raped his daughter, Beatrice. Together with her step-mother and remaining brothers, Beatrice successfully plotted the murder of her father. He was killed by hired assassins; a nail was hammered in one eye, and another in his throat. The plot was revealed and the conspirators were brought to trial. Pope Clement VII refused to pardon them, and on 11 September 1599, Beatrice, less than sixteen years old, and her mother and brother, Giacomo, were beheaded.

Artaud asked the painter Balthus Klossowski de Rola to create the decors and costumes for what he considered to be a metaphysical drama. He was attracted to Balthus' paintings because they revealed a certain violence and had at the same time, a tenderness and hypnotic intensity about them; the objects and people depicted frequently seemed like the materialisation of dreams and fantasies, giving them the impression of being detached from the 'outer world' event.

It is no wonder that the sets for *The Cenci* were arresting. A spiral gallery had been so constructed as to give the illusion of limitless depth and height. Subtle rhythmic effects are brought into play by the image of these unending circular spirals. A feeling of giddiness envelops both the actors and spectators as each is swept along in constant and continual rotation. This circular motion forces the audience to loose all perspective and balance, ushering it, gently at first, into a bizarrely exciting world. The spectator then becomes aware of the fact that mystical forces or powers are at work, that 'gravitation' is operating, and that objects and people are forever being refashioned and transformed in this drama of tragedy and gore.

Artaud had great hopes for *The Cenci*, but it ran for only seventeen days. It was, of course, a financial failure and the critics were nearly unanimous in their condemnation of the play. This drama, for Artaud was a Theatre of Cruelty play. It was comparable to a plague, he suggested, a disorder of the most horrendous type which brings with it both social and psychological disturbances. Such a disease, symbolically speaking, unleashes a 'spontaneous' or 'psychic fire', during which time people are no longer in control of their energies or emotions, which seem to cascade forth. This release of energy, which forces out passions of all types (incest, sexual abnormalities, and so forth), provoking horror and vertigo in the hearts of audiences, leads to a collective expulsion or regurgitation, followed by a collective purification. The tremendous 'flames' or 'luminescent suns', as Artaud called them, that people discharge either during a theatrical performance or during moments of great stress (as in a plague) are the same ones that they later transform in their fantasies into symbols and then into works of art.[8]

Antonin Artaud

Artaud had sought, unsuccessfully, to break the conventions of contemporary theatre and to obey the dictates of an 'inner necessity'. He had tried to dislocate the reality to which audiences were accustomed in the hope that they might achieve a deeper and more forthright way of considering life. Stage life, for Artaud, was a 'continuation' of real life and a search for meaning. His Alfred Jarry Theatre was a failure, as were all his other theatrical ventures. People scoffed at his 'metaphysical' and unworkable notions. He himself even became the butt of satire and ridicule, looked upon as an 'eccentric,' a clown, a jester.

In his time, Artaud was a man alienated from society, divided within himself, a victim of inner and outer forces beyond his control; and he remained isolated in an indifferent world. The tidal force of his imagination, the urgency of his therapeutic quest, were disregarded and cast aside. Today things have changed. What had been Artaud's individual situation has become a collective malady, and only a generation later.

It is difficult to define the *precise* influence Artaud's seminal ideas have had on contemporary authors, directors, and actors. In Jean Genet's *The Blacks* and *The Balcony* for example, religious atmosphere and ritual are of primary importance. In Beckett's *Waiting for Godot* and *End Game* archetypal characters use the densest language and action is symbolic. Eugene Ionesco's *The Bald Soprano* and *The Chairs* are, for the most part, allegories in which a shattering of language patterns gives words the force and presence of concrete objects. Fernando Arrabal's *Fando and Lis*, *The Automobile Graveyard* reveal the most secret fantasies as a series of grotesque creatures emerging full-grown from his subliminal sphere. Jean Vauthier's *Captain Bada, The Character Against Himself* uses a spatial language very similar to what Artaud advocated: sound

81

effects, objects, accessories, and lighting are given volatile personalities of their own, in order to arouse and disturb the spectator. Liliane Atlan's *Mister Fugue*, *The Carriage of Flames and Voices* does likewise by returning to her religious roots. Harold Pinter (*The Homecoming, The Birthday Party*) pays particular attention to verbal patterns, which he uses to intensify the tensions of his instinctual, fractured characters. Arnold Wesker (*The Kitchen*) drawn to fables, employs Artaud-like sound effects extensively. Edward Albee (*The Zoo Story, Who's Afraid of Virginia Woolf*) has a penchant for the shocking language and situations Artaud advocated. The more socially oriented Günter Grass (*The Tin Drum, The Wicked Cooks*) is drawn to elliptical stage happenings, jarring sounds, and bizarre visual patterns to shake the spectator's complacency, as was Peter Weiss (*Marat/Sade, The Investigation*). Peter Schaffer's *The Royal Hunt of the Sun* is a virtual transposition of Artaud's metaphysical drama *The Conquest of Mexico*.

Directors also have been affected by Artaud's aura – directly and indirectly. Roger Blin, who worked with Artaud and directed plays by Genet and Beckett, was prone to emphasise sets, lighting, and gestures as well as a work's metaphysical aspects. Michael Cacoyannis (*Iphigenia, Mourning Becomes Electra*) accords extreme importance to stylised acting, choreography, and sound effects. When Peter Hall directed *The Homecoming*, he enhanced its mystery and horror by creating a series of mobile stage images and using gestures and words as the repositories of arcane contents. *Marat/Sade*, as directed by Peter Brook, became a horrendous drama – a dance – in which all theatrical forces (visual, aural, sentient) were mustered in order to arouse a visceral reaction.

Artaud knew that in the end, his ideas would not only be

accepted but would be used to expand the spectators' reality by arousing the explosive and creative forces within their unconscious, an area he considered more powerful than the rational conscious in determining people's actions. By means of a theatre based on myths, symbols, and gestures, the play became an instrument for whipping up the audience's irrational forces, so that a collective theatrical event could be turned into a personal and living experience.

PART II
FARCE, COMEDY, SATIRE

Farce, comedy, and satire are implicit in the orgiastic and ribald but also painfully tragic works of the Flemish dramatists Fernand Crommelynck and Michel de Ghelderode. The Dionysiac quality of the laughter elicited by their boisterous satire of established institutions, expressed through the use of monomaniacal and frequently pathological characters, is arresting. The progressively distorted vision of humanity, the suspicious and demented miscreants obsessed by an *idée fixe*, render the two farce-comedies under discussion here – Crommelynck's *The Magnificent Cuckold* and Ghelderode's *Escurial* – unique visionary, auditory, and theatrical experiences.

Crommelynck and Ghelderode are master craftsmen. With the wizardry of the true artist, they transform the logic of the life experience into a grossly de-natured and absurd sequence of situations. As their bile-drenched pens discredit and destroy the so-called pillars of society, relatively

normal conditions degenerate onstage into horrific night-
mares. Dialect, neologisms, rhyme schemes, alliterations,
slang, and vernacular are all used in a variety of patterns to
point up character traits (jealously, envy, gluttony, demen-
tia, cowardice, and the like); while kicking, tumbling,
miming, dancing, running, and jumping underscore the
visual and sensuous qualities of their works. Coarse and
comic though their farce-comedies may be, they also
appeal to the intellect because of the abrasive nature of the
satire and irony incorporated into the characterisations and
themes.

5
Fernand Crommelynck
(1886–1970)

Fernand Crommelynck's theatre is neither a civic festival nor a morality lesson, nor is it designed for relaxation. It is a theatre of action, of psychological probings, of character evolution, of dramatic climaxes, and of shattering suspense scenes. The bizarre machinations of his protagonists, their instinctuality and crudeness, bring to mind the seventeenth-century *farceurs*. The young Molière, it has been claimed, was attracted to the Pont Neuf to observe the antics and verbal routines of the famous Tabarin, who would abash his viewers with his exaggerated visual and auditive compositions. Crommelynck captures the rudimentary temperament of the *farceur* in *The Magnificent Cuckold* (*Le Cocu magnifique*, 1920) and *Golden Tripe* (*Tripes d'Or*, 1925); and the lithe and imaginative quality of the *commedia dell'arte* plays with their improvisations and stock characters in *Carine* (1929); the hermetic implications of the mask in *The Sculptor of Masks* (*Le*

Sculpteur de Masques, 1911); the symbolic and illusory realm in *The Puerile Lovers* (*Les Amants puérils*, 1921); the more popular blends of boulevard theatre in *Hot and Cold* (*Chaud et Froid*, 1934) and *A Woman Whose Heart is too Small* (*La Femme qu'a le coeur trop petit*, 1934). To the innovations of his forerunners, Crommelynck adds his own spice and ironic overtones. Although Crommelynck's goal is to amuse, he also follows Hamlet's suggestion to the players, 'to hold, as 'twere, the mirror up to nature!'

Fernand Crommelynck was born in Paris of an acting family. When he was still young his parents moved to Belgium, and it was there that he discovered he had a flair for acting and writing. He returned to Paris prior to World War I, where he pursued his career as dramatist, actor, and journalist.[1]

Crommelynck's farces are not happy; indeed, they are touched with tragedy. In this respect they are in keeping with Ionesco's definition of the tragic farce: stage happenings of a violent, cruel, and absurd nature. For Ionesco, logic must be disrupted by the onslaught of improbable situations, eliciting nonsensical activity and unbelievable coincidences, and terminating with a crescendo of virulence. Crommelynck's tragi-comedies reveal a crumbling and disintegrating society whose values hamper human evolution rather than encourage it. His world is peopled with grotesque characters making their plight known through horrendous outbursts. Absurd and unreal qualities enter into the frenetic antics of the protagonists; but, as in the delirious fantasy of Armand Salacrou's *Breaker of Plates*, humour clothes an underlying spirit of anguish and revulsion. Crommelynck's protagonists are jealous, frequently without reason; they live in a fantasy realm that makes reality painful to face. With the introduction of the absurd and the unreal into the stage happenings, anything can take place in the illogical world of the obsessed.

'The Magnificent Cuckold', 1920

The performance of *The Magnificent Cuckold* at the Théâtre de l'Oeuvre, under the direction of Lugné-Poë, made theatrical history. Its success was accredited to the truculence and verve of its dialogue, the theme of jealousy transformed into a perversion, and Lugné-Poë's subtle interpretation of the protagonist.[2]

The play opens on a country scene: a converted windmill, the dream cottage of the newly married Stella and Bruno. The beautiful and demure young Stella stands in front of her home, singing to the birds and flowers, as she awaits the return of her poet-husband. A cowherd approaches her stealthily, unnoticed at first. When he begins making advances and attempts to carry her off, Stella's nurse rushes out of the house and helps her mistress fight off the intruder. Moments after the cowherd has left, the village count arrives and attempts unsuccessfully to win the young bride's affection. But Stella loves Bruno and remains faithful to him.

The mood suddenly changes when the peasant-like Bruno, naive and insensitive to the feelings of others, returns with Petrus, Stella's handsome young cousin. Unsolicited, Bruno, a romantic at heart, begins a rapturous poetical tirade about his wife's physical and spiritual beauty, going into panegyrics about a birthmark she has that is located in a very embarrassing place – which he mentions outright! His idealisation of his wife's pulchritude stuns those around her. This is only the beginning of his remarks on the subject. Now that he has apprised everyone of Stella's 'divine' beauty, Bruno wants to prove the veracity of his remarks, and he asks her to raise her skirts, unbutton her blouse, and show off her breasts to Petrus. Stella is abashed by such a request, but she is a good wife who seeks to please her husband and she acquiesces. When Bruno notices a flicker of passion on Petrus' eye – a perfectly normal reaction to such a vision – he has an uncontrollable outburst of temper and strikes Petrus. It is at this point that Lugné-Poë allows madness to emerge on the stage, as jealousy begins to erode his character's being. Breathless, tempestuous, Bruno asks his best friend Estrugo, the village scribe, to confirm Stella's fidelity. But even before a reply is forthcoming, Bruno concludes in the negative.

Bruno's wrath increases in Act II. He even accuses the angelical Stella of telling monstrous lies and of having a secret lover. Gesticulating virtually uncontrollably as he walks up and down the stage, Bruno allows his obsession free reign; he has contrived a variety of traps to catch his wife, and is, not surprisingly, unsuccessful every time. His uncertainty drives him to desperate measures. He goes so far as to ask Petrus to have sexual relations with Stella. He reasons that if he finds her with a lover or two, he will believe the opposite of what he observes and she will be able to prove her innocence. Petrus refuses Bruno's request; finally he acquiesces. 'Be cuckold he who wants to be.' Stilled at this point, Bruno asks Estrugo to look through the keyhole and report what occurs between Petrus and Stella. Estrugo follows orders. In keeping with this reverse-reality reasoning, Bruno is now convinced of his wife's innocence.

Estrugo is one of Crommelynck's finest caricatures. A blend of folly, wit, liveliness, fun, and stupidity, he is reminiscent of the stock character Bucco (Mouth) of Atellan satiric drama. Estrugo keeps prattling throughout the scene, but Bruno never believes him, and Estrugo's verbal transcriptions become the catalyst of Bruno's own destruction. Estrugo was, for Crommelynck, an 'ambiguous double', a kind of devil figure; costumed in whiteface and sneakers, he employs stylised gestures to excel as a mime. His observations, transcribed by the fervour of his gestures, succeed not in depicting the truth of the situation but in substantiating Bruno's accusations and insinuations. Estrugo details the activities taking place between Petrus and Stella. As he looks through the keyhole, he reports upon the sexual activities both verbally and visually, miming the scene in part, expressing his indignation and impatience by bouncing up and down from a seated position to a lying one, thrusting his hands in front of him in despair or rapture, and casting his eyes to the ground in dismay and perhaps a kind of ecstasy. Whatever the manoeuvres, his plastic gymnastics fail to convince Bruno of Stella's innocence. Estrugo – the Mouth and the Mime – become Bruno's vehicle for self-destruction, his escape mechanism.

Crommelynck moulds his characters to fit into their phallus-obsessed world, underscoring in the most outlandish terms the lengths to which their twisted views may be carried. When Bruno, for example, is convinced that Stella is planning a tryst with an unknown lover, he forces her to wear a dark cloak and an ugly cardboard mask which hide her completely. She stands out in sharp contract with the colourful and lively peasant costumes worn by the other participants. Her accessories make her unappetising. The weight of the mask and cloak render her stance awkward and ungainly, repelling the men of her entourage. Gone is the beautiful and joyous *commedia dell'arte* ingenue.

Feelings of hostility, anxiety, uncertainty, and fear are aroused by Crommelynck's reverse-reality procedure and in contemporary performances were heightened by Lugné-Poë's extraordinarily vivid facial expressions, which ranged from jolly country bumpkin to vicious pervert. The candid charm, the tenderness, the touching grace of Stella at the outset of the drama are tarnished by Bruno's aberration, disturbed by the nightmarish quality of his lugubrious world.

In Act III, in scenes unrivalled in French theatre for their mad hilarity, Bruno attempts to prove further his wife's fidelity. He forces her to give herself to many young men. Although he sees them pawing and petting her in public, and this on the stage in 1920 was virtually unheard of in serious theatre, Bruno is still convinced he is not a cuckold. Would she indulge so openly in sexual activities if she were guilty, he questions. He rationalises that she could not. In keeping with his insane views, Bruno asks the young men to be more tender to her. Estrugo cannot believe that Bruno is allowing this situation to persist. When the burgomaster and townswomen realise what is taking place in Bruno's home, they demand that this scandalous activity cease at once. Tired of trying to prove her love to her husband, Stella informs him finally that she is leaving him for the cowherd, whom she kisses on the mouth as Bruno watches in disbelief. Bruno's fantasy has become reality; but his insanity is such that he now believes his wife's departure is but another huge joke and he bursts into guffaws.

Crommelynck's expert use of caricature enables him to heighten or to slacken the play's pace, therefore controlling its suspense. He stresses the *lazzi* aspects of *The Magnificent Cuckold*: extreme action that forever generates excitement and sparks madness. When the cowherd enters, the idyllic and romantic opening lines suddenly change to hectic activity. Stella is forced to fight off the intruder. The rough-and-tumble gestures that ensue (always centred around the phallus-oriented desires) are so speedily enacted, including clouts bandied about, that a kaleidoscopic atmosphere is achieved. These serve to underscore the extreme activity in modern society. When the count comes after Stella, another, less lively, stage battle ensues in which the elegance of the count's gestures and Stella's earthy manner set off a plebeian versus aristocratic approach to sex. Speed and an overt sense of jocularity are achieved again in the last act when the young men of the village run after Stella and tear at her clothes, expressing the urgency of their desires. They are truly the inheritors of the Greek *comus*: theirs is a veritable celebration of earthy ways expressed through leaping and running incited by sexual frenzy.

Lugné-Poë transformed Bruno during the course of the play into a libidinous lecher, a 'giant, erotic clown', a 'sexually obsessed' individual who was forever 'eating Stella with his eyes' and 'beating her while trembling with wantonness'.[3] Lugné-Poë understood the morbid side of a man who had become prey to demons, who had stepped over that 'shadowy line' from sanity to madness. It was for this reason that some of his ripostes were spoken with such force as to resemble a series of 'striking fist marks' aimed at both protagonists and spectators. Variety, too, was implicit in his portrayal: there were moments of desperate lyricism, deep emotion, and a tenderness that 'verged on the sublime'.[4]

The Moscow production in 1922 of *The Magnificent Cuckold*, directed by Vsevolod Meyerhold, with sets by L. P. Popova, was praised in newspapers the world over for its innovations in acting techniques, stage design, lighting, and directing. Meyerhold's production stressed the humour and boldness of caricature, while simultaneously underscoring the world of illusion and earthiness. The Russian director rejected the realistic theatre of Stanislavsky in favour of a new reality that sought to arouse the spectators' emotions and imagination. For Meyerhold, theatre was not designed merely to entertain an aristocratic public, rather he sought to concretise the revolutionary goals of the new Russia. To achieve this effect, he abolished the stage curtain, as had Lugné-Poë and Paul Fort in France. He extended, as they had, the proscenium arch out into the audience so that a closer interchange could take place between spectator and actor. He also constructed, as had Jacques Copeau, mobile forms on a bare stage in lieu of decors, accentuating the temporal quality of the atmosphere. He rejected suspended decors and theatrical arches and so allowed action to take place outside the 'scenic cage'. As with Copeau, for Meyerhold each play was an individual blending of gesture, movement, and speech. His method, described as the 'technique of biomechanics', is set forth as follows. 'The whole technique of biomechanics lies in the careful study of the time of preparation for a certain action; of the emotional and physical state of the moment of action itself; and the resulting anticlimax of reaction.'[5] Gestures and body movements had to be precise and in keeping with the personality portrayed. The intonations and emerging emotions would then find their natural equivalents and the actors would be able to coordinate the means at their disposal to express their character's 'excitability'.[6]

Meyerhold used his acting area three-dimensionally: the actor was no longer isolated on the stage but participated in the general flow of rhythmic and spatial dynamics generated by a harmonious combination of body, scenery, and accessories. His directives to L. P. Popova, the creator of the stage apparatus for *The Magnificent Cuckold*, resulted in a display of the restless energy inherent in Crommelynck's protagonists.

Popova was a Constructivist. Unlike the Cubists, who broke down objects in terms of form and used movement as a means of expressing mass, the Constructivists were anti-aesthetic. They used raw materials for their creations, which were designed to be functional and utilitarian, blending political beliefs ('the soul and ideals of the workers') with artistic creativity. Constructivism originated in Russia around 1913 and its main supporters were Malevich, Tatlin, Rodchenko, and Popova. Its practitioners produced designs consisting of circles, diagonals, and rectangles applied to a blank background. Each design was to impress itself into the spatial form in question in perfect proportion and balance, each line representing an organic mass in terms of motion, colour, and texture.[7]

For *The Magnificent Cuckold* the stage setting was based on the following principles outlined by Meyerhold:

1. Three-dimensional linear construction.
2. Visual rhythm determined by effects that were neither pictorial nor set in relief.
3. The inclusion in the construct of only those 'active' parts necessary for the actor's activities.[7]

In order to situate the scene in some temporal domain, Meyerhold suggested that Popova build a wheel, since Crommelynck's stage directions said that the play took place in a converted windmill. The lively colours Popova used in the design of the wheel would help audiences and actors experience the rotary sensation of the mill while giving the entire scene a kaleidoscopic effect.

Popova's construct consisted of black, white, and red multiform pedestals made up of circles, stairs, ladders, doors, squares, rectangles, and parallels. Each was an organic entity in itself, each an expression of the actor's kineticism, each organising space in terms of rhythmic and plastic dimensions. The stage was active and diametrically opposed to the conventional decors used in Parisian productions. Lighting focused only on the stage areas where activity occurred, opposing light and dark spatial areas, which injected a greater dynamism into the proceedings. The actors wore mainly the working-man's blue apron, but other 'work clothes' and distinguishing accessories were added to each character's costume, as Meyerhold specified, in keeping with his role.

Popova's large and complicated stage apparatus was used in its entirety when groups filled the proscenium, and in separate sections when one or two actors came on stage. As the actors jumped, fell, or disappeared, they performed on the various parts of the construct, which was superbly adaptable. Each element of the setting played a dual role: as a single bench, window, incline, or other elements, and as part of a totality – the massive object viewed as a whole.

Popova's scheme was in perfect keeping with the ebullience of the protagonists' adolescent psyches. Viewed either as a utilitarian object to serve actors and playwrights or as a giant toy to mirror the protagonists' anthropoid psyches, it remained a memorable achievement in theatre design.

Meyerhold's emphasis on the visual dimension of *The Magnificent Cuckold* created a kind of macro-structure in which the protagonists lived their solitary as well as their collective roles. The new universe that came into being, an agglomeration of figurations, was action personified, triggering off a continuous series of emotional collisions. The spectacle became an awakening process through visual experience as well as the word.

The Magnificent Cuckold remained Crommelynck's

greatest success. George Pioch called it 'a work of genius;' Maurice Rostand, 'unique in the annals of the theatre,' one of 'the most powerful studies in jealousy;' and Marcel Lapierre, 'a play of monumental proportion.'[8]

6
Michel de Ghelderode
(1898–1962)

For Ghelderode, theatre is a dangerous art, as are 'all great and authentic passions', for it leads to the unknown and to the invisible. Spectres people his world in *Escurial*; they manifest themselves in semi-human creatures who indulge in frantic farcelike activity. With the rigid faces, frozen grimaces, and congealed grins of the marionette, these instinctive beings are not the products of reason, but emerge spasmodically from Ghelderode's primordial depths. They are forever attempting to free themselves from some ingrained and hereditary fear, some archaic sense of morality and social order, but rarely, if ever, do they succeed in liberating themselves from their inhibitions, their constrictions.

Ghelderode's plays delineate different phases involved in the decomposition of personalities, exposing in the process the nuances of decay. Few if any of his characters are endowed with vision; fewer still have the strength to battle for their ideas and to pave the way for inner evolution. Their feeble natures and unhealthy psyches, as well as the insalubrious conditions surrounding them, impede normal growth. Their world is black, but it is not the rich blackness which offers a full range of harmoniously blended nutrients. Ghelderode's mixtures breed ghouls and gnomes, monsters with distorted souls. His creatures befoul the air they breathe, revel in their own decay, delight in their sadomasochistic behaviour, grimace and screech; all rejoice in their sexual perversions. Reminiscent of the emanations of a Bosch, Grünewald, Brueghel, Ensor, or Goya's depictions of crazed beings, Ghelderode's excrescences are stunted, malformed, degenerate.

Ghelderode's monsters disrupt and disorient, but they never resolve the chaos in their hearts. Instead, each brings about further deterioration, greater ruin and despair. The central character in *The Death of Doctor Faustus* (*La Mort du Docteur Faustus*, 1925) is not Goethe's Faust, a man whose descent culminates in redemption, but an anti-hero who fails religiously, philosophically, and socially. A neurasthenic, Ghelderode's Faust sees no positive way in life and takes no affirmative stand. Only microbes exist in *Don Juan* (1928). Love is based on the lie. It is an illusion created by human beings to help them escape from the horrors of life. *Christopher Columbus* (1927) dramatises the plight of the idealist-poet who dreams of adventure and beauty and instead becomes the prey of a covetous and ungrateful populace dominated by political and religious fanatics. *Barabbas* (1928) demonstrates the futility of sacrifice. Nothing positive can come through sacrifice, since nothing can stop humanity's lust for maiming and killing. *Pantagleize* (1939) dramatises the fate of the creative person: the sensitive and innocent poet is devoured by society. *Chronicles of Hell* (*Fastes d'Enfer*,

1929) focuses on death: a poisoned host, a noxious idea, individuals and societies killed. The miser's saga unfolds in *Red Magic* (*Magie Rouge*, 1931). Gold, around which the spiritual and the physical revolve, absorbs Ghelderode's hero, who finally couples with his shekels. *Lord Halweyn* (1934) delineates the antics of an impotent man who takes pleasure in blood and gore.

A medieval tone is implicit in all of Ghelderode's plays. He had always been absorbed in things of the past. His father, a clerk at the General Archives in Brussels, where Michel was born, encouraged him to study ancient documents, genealogies, history books, and engravings of all types.[1] His fascination with the past may also have resulted in part from a bout with typhus in 1915, which necessitated his withdrawal from school. Deep-seated introversion followed, and became a hallmark of Ghelderode's character. After some desultory studies at the Conservatoire Royal de Musique, he started writing articles for the financial weekly *Mercredi-Bourse*, which allowed him to earn a meagre living. Throughout these years the young lad spent much of his leisure time haunting marionette theatres. He was mesmerised by wooden puppets; those 'supernatural' and sometimes satanic beings fired his imagination, parading their terrors in a cruelly humorous vein.

'Escurial' (1927)

Renaissance Spain provided the setting for *Escurial*, which opened in Paris in 1948 under the direction of René Dupuy, who also played the part of Folial. It earned rave reviews from critics in the know, but not, obviously, from the general public, who either ignored its presence or who simply did not understand what it was all about. *Escurial* was not a boulevard play; it was, however, a work of art which reflected Ghelderode's penchant for the lugubrious unregenerate forces within humankind's subliminal world.

Escurial was also a vehicle which allowed Dupuy to disclose his histrionic talents as Folial the buffoon. As for the seasoned actor Michel Vitold, his portrayal of the sadistic and insane king was considered extraordinary for its depth, for the remarkable manner in which he built up tension to the breaking point.

Escurial was named after a palace built near Madrid by Philip II in 1557, after defeating the French at Saint-Quentin. It housed a rich library, paintings by El Greco, a convent, and a college. Philip II lived in only one of the rooms in Escurial. It was virtually devoid of furniture and opened on two alcoves: a study and a bedroom with a slit in the wall which allowed the king to follow from his bed the religious services held in an adjoining chapel. Philip II died in Escurial.

A colossal worker, Philip II, was endowed with a powerful personality. Sombre and introverted, he surrounded himself with darkness; he even clothed himself in black. His shadow spread death and ruin wherever it was cast. Although the Holy Inquisition had been established earlier in Spain by Ferdinand and Isabella (1492), Philip was instrumental in furthering its power. He encouraged the clergy and the military to seek out Jews, Moors, or anyone accused of heresy, either to convert them or to burn them at the stake. Murder and horror marked his reign. It was Ghelderode's fascination with this lugubrious and sordid being that inspired him to write his play.

'Think of painting,' Ghelderode wrote his director when Dupuy was preparing the mise-en-scène for *Escurial*. The playwright particularly had in mind El Greco's canvas of

King John which was hanging in the Louvre in Paris: 'haggard, visibly degenerate, and pulmonary, in brief, a kind of clinical specimen'. This vision was also meant to inspire Vitold, who would be portraying the king onstage: 'a terrible, disquieting, unforgettable being', who had haunted the Belgian dramatist ever since he saw the canvas in 1925.[2]

Escurial opens on a dimly lit room surrounded by a maze of dismal and drafty corridors and chambers. The sets are simple: a wobbly throne perched on top of four rickety steps surrounded by black drapes. The carpets leading to the throne are threadbare. 'It is the throne of a madman wrapped in funereal solitude', Ghelderode wrote, 'the last vestige of a dying and noble race'. As the curtains part, the king is slumped over his throne, and is 'moaning wretchedly'.[3]

Ghelderode frequently accentuated the destructive and negative inner climate of his protagonists through his lighting effects and decor; *Escurial* is no exception to the rule. The stage directions call for an eerie 'subterranean' light, which mirrors the king's fear of being overthrown and his horror of sterility and impotence. The deteriorating furnishings stress the unregenerate nature of the ruling principle. The stage room takes on the dimensions and contours of a cave. Let us recall that cave cults were popular in ancient times. Sybils and oracles inhabited these dark and remote regions and from them predicted their events. Christian martyrs also found serenity in such womb-like enclosures. As for Philip II, he rarely left his room after he grew old. The atmosphere in *Escurial* is sickly. No air is allowed to flow, emphasising the claustrophobic nature of the king's world, which can only lead to further decomposition.

As the play begins, audiences view an anguished, skeletal

king, dressed in red and black rags. He is cupping his ears, attempting to shut out the deafening sounds of barking dogs and also to symbolically deny the reality they force upon him: his queen is about to die. In most mythologies, dogs are associated with the underworld, with forces that guide people to the realm of the dead. In *Escurial*, they are harbingers of death and not the positive and faithful creatures associated with Saint Roch or the Dominican order (*Domini canes*, 'dogs of the Lord'). As creatures of the night, dogs serve to blend with and prolong the sordid atmosphere of the play.

Bells are also sounded, intoning mournful notes. Always important for Ghelderode, a man so sensitive to music, bells evoked for him medieval and Renaissance polyphonic compositions, and their primordial vibrations were a prelude to human and divine activities. In *Escurial*, bells speak their own language in subtle cosmic rhythms, disclosing the anguish of an afflicted heart.

The collective tonalities of the bells and the howling of the dogs create both a celestial and infernal music, a composite of conflicting emotions, rhythms, and sonorities. In the stage production, bells succeed in prolonging and fleshing out the religious and sinister atmosphere which marked Philip II's reign. They are so significant that the livid tubercular-looking monk who later makes his appearance begs the king to let him sound them. 'It would be an immense charity, a saintly action to let the bells ring . . . bells announce Heavenly and terrestrial joys and pains.' The king relents. He knows he is powerless against an implacable destiny. And just as the bells howled and wailed in medieval mystery dramas, counting the hours of Christ's agony, marking its progression, so they replicate the dying queen's torment, and by extension that of the king's clown-buffoon, Folial.

Like Philip II, Ghelderode's king is a lonely being; a 'night spirit' with a shadow personality and the smile of a satiated vampire. Ghelderode's king is also cruel and rigid, and sinful in the sense that he is absorbed by possessiveness, intransigence, and hatred, never loosening his stranglehold on those whom he considers his enemies. Ghelderode's genius lies in part in his ability to dramatise the king's subliminal world to bring the myopic creatures that people his inner domain into the open and compel his audiences to experience their chaos.

The king, victimised by fear, calls for Folial to entertain him. (Inspired by Velasquez's magnificent dwarf 'bloated with blood and instincts', Dupuy, who played this grotesque apparition in the 1948 production, was striking as he attempted but failed to comply with the king's order to make him laugh.) Although Folial is dressed in the colourful attire of a buffoon, his entire demeanour mirrors the hue of pain. He loved the queen and was loved by her. Now that she is about to die, he feels his sorrow too acutely even to pretend to amuse his master. The king threatens him with death unless he obeys. Folial acquiesces and suggests they enact a farce together. In Belgium, farces are traditionally performed during Lent. Someone is chosen to assume the power and authority of a great monarch. When he is fully bloated with pride, the populace uncrowns and deflates him. The merriment of such a ritual is derived from the destruction of the powerful ruling force in the community.

The farce begins. Folial grabs the king's crown and sceptre and assumes a regal stance. He then wraps his hands around the monarch's neck. His grip tightens. The king's strident cackle disorients him, and Folial loosens his grip. The king is delighted. He is enjoying the game. When he plays the buffoon, the king begins to jump, laugh,

grimace, whirl about, and then dance. 'I dance my libera-
tion,' says the king, 'I dance like a widower, like a goat on a
witches' sabbath, like an old satyr.'

Dancing, the most primitive of instinctual expressions, is
humanity's way of becoming reabsorbed into the atmosphere about them. The circles the dancer weaves around
the stage result in a loss of equilibrium and individual
identity. Once a fixed position or view of life has been
uprooted, a reblending may occur; new and fresh com-
ponents may emerge. But such is not the king's case. The
king's dance allows him to expel his hatred, lust, and anger,
but only temporarily. These emotions once again flood his
being, dimming his vision.

Pausing, the king accuses Folial of having committed the
seven deadly sins and other 'abominations'. The number
seven is identified in *Escurial* with negative attributes, as is
everything else in the drama; never are the seven virtues
mentioned. The king associates his buffoon with absolute
evil and with the devil. 'I love you for your perfection in
evil', he tells him.

To underscore the decidedly uncomfortable condition of
his protagonists and add to the play's visceral impact upon
the audience, Ghelderode has recourse to images of skulls,
fleas, carion, and larvae. The Latin word *larva* means
'ghost'; in Roman times larvae were thought to be evil
spirits that wandered about graveyards and near criminals,
grimacing and cackling as they made their way about in
darkness, terrorising young and old. In *Escurial*, the king
asks Folial whether his 'cranium is filled with larvae', thus
denigrating his thought processes and arousing further
feelings of revulsion.

The king suggests to Folial that they carry their game a
step further. He asks Folial to don his vestments while he
puts on the jester's. Folial walks up the throne in full

regalia. The crown of gold which is exchanged between the king and Folial during the farce episode is considered, symbolically, as the most splendid of objects. It is God's mouthpiece and the sun's earthly counterpart. Since the crown is placed on the head, it reaches closest to heaven; in that it is made of the noblest and purest of metals, its rays shine throughout the cosmos, shedding light – the highest expression of enlightenment and spirituality. The sceptre, which is also exchanged between the king and Folial, is a paradigm of authority, power, and justice. The transference of crown and sceptre during the farce implies that the ruling authority is no longer a stable force, that it dispenses neither justice nor any governing power, that it has lost solid footing. Rulership, then, is unsteady; stability and harmony are toppling. The edifice is about to crumble.

During the farcical interlude, the king, playing the role of the buffoon, confesses his suffering and the jealousy he experienced when discovering his wife's love for Folial. He tells Folial also that the queen has been poisoned, 'The farce is over'. When the king asks Folial to return his crown and sceptre, his identity, Folial refuses. He attempts to strangle the king, but fails in his endeavour. A white-faced monk enters and informs the king of his wife's death. 'You love Death,' the king tells the monk, 'its odour and its splendour!' Folial is stunned. Taking advantage of his shock, the king grabs the symbols of authority and calls for the executioner. Dressed in scarlet and wearing a hood which allows only his eyes and nose to be seen, the executioner enters and strangles Folial. The king bursts out in hysterical laughter.

Folial failed to achieve dominion over the king. Such defeat is understandable since the root of his name indicates 'fool'; or 'madman' (*fou, fol* in French). He lacked the necessary mental attributes to assume power.

His momentary exchange of identity with the king was not sufficient to establish a new ruling principle. The thinking function, so well developed in the king, was dormant in Folial. His feelings were forever surging forth and disconcerting him at the most inappropriate moments. Since they had been experienced only on a subliminal level, in secret, dark, and remote corners of the palace, and thus on unconscious rather than conscious levels, they remained undeveloped, infantile, and ineffective. Twice Folial could have killed the king; twice his feelings intruded and prevented him from completing his act. He loosened his grip around the king's neck when he heard his strident laughter and then when he was told of the queen's death. Rather than attempting to understand Folial's contempt for what he represents, the king enjoys his buffoon's game of strangulation. He delights in his hatred of him and admires the power in his hands. In time, he muses, Folial could even become a good executioner.

When Folial fails to strangle him, however, the king loses respect for the buffoon. He derides the fact that Folial's feelings dominate and not his reason. 'Worry, anguish, despair' appear on his face and not on the king's, where they rightfully belong. Folial is so weakly structured that when he is attired in the king's vestments and ordered to mount the throne, he barely has the strength to walk up the few steps. The crown and sceptre weigh too heavily upon him. The love and beauty he once knew, which helped him find momentary fulfillment, no longer exist.

When the king, in Folial's clothes, announces the queen's death by poison and pursues his chatter in the most cavalier manner, informing Folial that another wife will be found with great ease, he prances about the stage and admits he was really born to be a clown. 'I grimace naturally; I am perfidious and dissimulate, like women in this respect.' His abandon seems complete as he begins to whirl about like 'an old satyre'. he is decidedly comfortable in the role he plays, 'My business is to wound.'

'After the farce, the tragedy,' the king declares at the play's finale. Laughter is Ghelderode's mask. It is his way of deriding humanity's earthly condition, of expelling his own hatred, boredom, and fear of sterility, and exposing his disillusionment and bitterness. As Paul Klee wrote, 'A laugh is mingled with the deep lines of pain.'

Escurial may be looked upon symbolically, as the dramatisation of a blood sacrifice (Folial's immolation) and the death of those functions (love and feeling) that he represents. The ruling principle, in the form of the king, survives: anger, hatred, and repression. Ghelderode's king should have been sacrificed, as was the case in ancient times when the old king (or the old year) was ceremoniously killed, thus insuring seasonal fertility. With the king's demise a separation of the prevailing conscious attitude would have given way to new blendings, new solutions. But this does not come to pass. Senescent views prevail and hate smothers love. Youth is destroyed, while old age pursues its narrow and destructive course.

The audience was stunned by what they called Ghelderode's 'macabre farce', reminiscent of Shakespeare because it 'attains a violence and majesty' unprecedented in contemporary drama. An 'extraordinary' evening in theatre, others wrote, bringing to mind the 'truculent' and 'sinister' emanations of a Bosch or Rouault. The 'remarkable' decors of Christiane Lenier were also mentioned: the throne, 'perched on the summit of four to five steps,' looked as though it were ready to topple any moment. As for the mad, sadistic king, devoured by fear and vice, Michel Vitold's portrayal was indelibly fixed in the mind's eye. His 'rage and bitterness,' his 'demoniacal nature' were revealed in subtle gestures, meaningful facial expressions, stances which seemed to have been lifted directly from Goya and Velasquez at their best. René Dupuy's Folial realised 'admirably the atrocity of his situation,' the progressive encroachment of the 'mortuary' atmosphere. Both actors, the critics suggested, underscored Ghelderode's 'admirably eloquent style'; and 'the plenitude of his phrasings'.[4]

There are no heroes in Ghelderode's plays; his characters represent a carnival of human folly in which vanity, egotism, and cruelty are brought forth in all their disquieting grandeur. Subtleties, understanding, and tenderness have been banished from the world of this dramatist, who is at the antipodes, as we shall see, of Giraudoux's golden realm and Anouilh's illusory domain. Ghelderode breathes life into nightmarish and fiendish ghouls, each wearing the gargoyle's smirk. His theatre flagellates in the most spectacular of ways!

PART III
MYTHIC THEATRE

We have grouped Cocteau's *Orpheus*, Giraudoux's *Ondine*
and Ohis *Madwoman of Chaillot*, Anouilh's *Traveller
Without Luggage*, and Claudel's *Break of Noon* under the
rubric 'mythic theatre'. These dramatists were not convention breakers; neither are their works plotless nor does the
irrational world reign, though some sequences and antics
are certainly absurd. Characters in the above-mentioned
dramas are identifiable to a certain extent with people in
the everyday world, as are the situations enacted. What is
innovative and of import is the mythic dimension of these
plays, their eternality.

What do we understand by mythic theatre? A myth may
be defined as a dramatic relating of those experiences or a
description of those qualities which are deepest within
humankind and certainly within the psyches of the authors
under scrutiny here. Myths are the outcome of original
experiences, not always personal, but sometimes impersonal or transcendental. The word *myth* (stemming from
muthos or 'fable',) implies the relating of an event or events

that transcend linear time, that speak to many generations, though the themes may appear to be timely ones. The plays chosen for scrutiny in this section also possess a religious dimension (*religio*, from the Latin, means 'linking back'), thus inviting both author and reader, or spectator, to live and relive the 'fabulous' events they recount, which took place in some real or fictional past.

Myths cannot be understood or explicated on an intellectual level alone, but must be experienced by the reader or spectator fully and viscerally, and the same is true for the dramas of Cocteau, Giraudoux, Anouilh, and Claudel. These plays arouse the ear with their poetry, the inner eye with their remarkable imagery, and the imagination with the exciting events they recount.

The Orpheus myth, for example, as dramatised by Cocteau, lives as a burning reality in the psyche of many. Cocteau sees himself in part as a modern Orpheus, a poet and bard struggling for inspiration which seems to be slipping from him; blaming his slackening élan on the demands made by women – viragos – and on a society equally oblivious to the needs of the creative individual.

Giraudoux's *Ondine* and his *Madwoman of Chaillot* are utopian myths, romantic in their ideology. The first deals with a water spirit, who symbolises all that is pure, honourable, and natural in life; who is unable to adapt to the hypocrisy and artificiality of court life. *Ondine* depicts the struggle between good and evil. Only an archetypal Madwoman of Chaillot, an insane force that lives on eternally in society, can safeguard integrity and beauty in modern times – elements so vital to a culture.

The hero in Anouilh's *The Traveller Without Luggage* is no Promethean. He is a hero grown old and wise. A war and amnesia separate the mature man from the self-centred and greedy adolescent that he was. The situation offers him the possibility of wiping the slate clean, of starting his life over again. The myth of renewal is, then, introduced within the framework of post-war life.

'I wrote it [*Break of Noon*] with my blood', Claudel confessed. The love he dramatised in his play centred around adultery, a catalytic force so powerful for him that the wound still smarted when Jean-Louis Barrault staged the work in 1948, forty-eight years after the event had taken place. To convey the immensity of the feelings involved, Claudel called the elements into play (sun, moon, water, earth, fire), compelling reader and audience to experience his passion both spiritually and viscerally. This adulterous love had brought him back to his roots, to a tremendous *mystery* which he lived and consummated.

Time in the mythic theatre of Cocteau, Giraudoux, Anouilh, and Claudel is reversible; reality, therefore, includes both the conscious and unconscious world, the temporal and atemporal domains. Endowed with that undefinable element which transcends the linear and visible world, *Orpheus, Ondine, The Madwoman of Chaillot, The Traveller Without Luggage*, and *Break of Noon* crackle with energy and excitement, offering audiences a new poetic language, fresh worlds which tingle and palpitate before them. Each viewer or reader is invited to see and experience life and the creative act in a wondrously moving and thrilling way, as a participant in the fabulation of a myth.

7
Jean Cocteau
(1889–1963)

Cocteau's *Orpheus* is a restatement of the ancient myth which imbued so many cultures with a sense of mystery and awe. In Cocteau's nimble fingers, however, the tragic Greek tale became a humorous and disturbing drama, focusing not on an ideal loving couple but on an 'infernal ménage'. The play, replete with puns and witticisms, introduces viewers and readers into a magical and mysterious world of cleverly manipulated symbols and images.

Cocteau was one of the first twentieth-century writers to restore Greek tragedy to modern audiences. His streamlined adaptations of *Antigone, Oedipus Rex*, and *The Infernal Machine* (*La Machine infernale*, 1934) based on the Oedipus myth, created a new style in French theatre. André Gide referred to this new direction as a kind of epidemic, an *Oedipémie*, and it was a trend which encouraged Jean Giraudoux and Jean Anouilh, among others, to follow.

Cocteau rejected the popular well-made play characteristic of the naturalist school, with its flesh-and-blood characters and its real-life props. This is not to say that he fled from realism into the arcane world of fantasy. On the contrary, Cocteau never tried to 'arrange' reality nor to 'attenuate' it; but rather to introduce a new vision of reality by accentuating it, as Ionesco was to do in *The Bald Soprano, The Lesson, The Chairs*, and other plays. Like Jarry, Apollinaire, and Artaud, Cocteau dehumanised his characters, rendering his theatre nonpsychological and as objective as possible. His creatures never existed on a personal level; they were types, functions, symbols, instincts, or inanimate objects. Each could be anyone and everyone: without identity or character as they plunged from one situation to another, never really coming to life as individuals, but remaining formless and amoeba-like amid the swirling sands of the collective world.

Since Cocteau's plays were non-psychological for the most part and possessed of no 'ordinary' plot, and since his characters were not socially oriented, he had to devise a new way of creating audience-actor empathy. He could not hope for the traditional type of projection on the part of the spectators: they could not possibly see themselves in the shadows and evanescent creatures onstage. He therefore had to force the spectators into becoming his accomplices. Influenced by Alfred Jarry in this technique, Cocteau rejected the concept of theatre as illusion by deliberately provoking audiences to laughter at the most unlikely moments: when Orpheus' head remained onstage after his death and answered to the name of Jean Cocteau. He also used traps, snares, magic, hoaxes, and shock techniques. In *The Infernal Machine*, for example, he had Jocasta, Oedipus's mother, talk to a common soldier in all-too-intimate terms while jazz blared away in the background. The queen's vulgarity destroyed any shred of empathy audiences might feel for her, and the ragtime music did away with all semblance of historicity in the drama. This premeditated use of unconventional techniques was calculated to startle audiences out of their usual conceptions of illusion and reality. They were lured into the author's new theatrical world and became accomplices in his 'game.' If they could not project or empathise with the characters, they could participate in the fantasies and the merrymaking, the ludic aspects of this macabre myth.

'I was born a Parisian, I speak Parisian, my accent is Parisian,' Cocteau wrote about the city which was to play such a vital and inspirational role in his creative life as a dramatist. In *Portraits-Souvenirs*, he recounts that he and his friends used to wait outside the theatre to see the famous actress Réjane emerge; her subtle portrayal in such plays as *Madame Sans-Gêne* by Victorien Sardou had earned her the admiration of many. Sarah Bernhardt had also been one of Cocteau's favourites. Indeed, she had already become a myth for all the world. Eccentric, passionate, self-willed, even cruel, she held Paris enthralled as she strode onstage as Phèdre, Hamlet, and l'Aiglon. But it was perhaps the aging lion of the Comédie-Française, Mounet-Sully, who left the most lasting impression on the young Cocteau. When gouging out his eyes in his portrayal of Oedipus, he assumed a sculptural quality, roared like a wild animal, and bounded around the stage, shaking his head in frenzied pain. Cocteau found music-hall stars equally beguiling, and circus life also beckoned.[1]

When Cocteau met Serge Diaghilev, founder of the Russian Ballet (1912), a new era in creativity opened up for him. A tireless worker who constantly searched for fresh talents and techniques, Diaghilev attracted to his fold such composers as Claude Debussy, Igor Stravinsky, Maurice Ravel, and the members of 'The Six' (Georges Auric,

Arthur Honegger, Darius Milhaud, Francis Poulenc, Germaine Taillefer, Louis Durey). The elegance of Diaghilev's production of *Scheherazade*, featuring the extraordinary Nijinsky, won immediate acclaim. Cocteau introduced Picasso to Diaghilev and from this meeting was born the fabulous ballet *Parade* (1917); the jarring colours and bizarre shapes of Picasso's costumes, the atonal music of Satie's composition; and the ambiguity of Cocteau's scenario were taken as insults by the audience. Sets and costumes no longer figured merely as background entities, but were transformed into formidable protagonists in *Parade*; they were accorded the same vital role in the larger than life-sized grotesque cardboard heads, masks, and costumes created by Raoul Dufy for Cocteau's pantomime, *The Do-Nothing Bar* (*Le Boeuf sur le toit*, 1920), the accessories in *The Wedding on the Eiffel Tower* (*Les Mariés de la Tour Eiffel*, 1921), and the sets in *Orpheus* (1932).

'Orpheus' (1926)

Ever since 1920, Cocteau had been intrigued by the Orpheus myth and had wanted to write a play based on the mythical son of the muse Calliope and a Thracian king (or Apollo). Orpheus was the greatest singer and musician of all time: the sounds he made when he played were so dazzling that they could make wild animals, trees, and even stones do what he desired.

Orpheus opened in Paris at the Théâtre des Arts on 17 June 1926. With Georges Pitoëff as director and playing Orpheus opposite his wife Ludmilla's Eurydice, success, as was to be expected, was a reality.[2] Indeed, the performance, the critics wrote, was electrifying. The theatre was filled to capacity with poets, painters, musicians, even the *Tout-Paris*. Still, many first-nighters were stunned. Was it

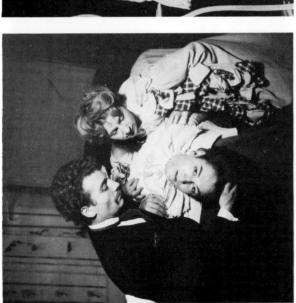

1. *Victor* at the Agnes Capri Theatre, 1946. Monique Lévrier, Michel de Ré, Ivan Penck.

2. *Victor*, Paris production, 1962. Monique Melinand, Claude Rich, Bernard Noël.

3. *Les Cenci*, 1935, Folies Wagram. Centre: Lady Abdy.

4. *Le Cocu Magnifique* directed by Vsevolod Meyerhold in Moscow in 1922, set designed by L. P. Popova.

5. *Le Cocu Magnifique*, 1922.

6. *Escurial*, Théâtre de L'Oeuvre, 1945. Rene Dupuy, Michel Vitold.

7. *Orphée* staged by Jean Leuvrais in Paris, 1963. Christiane Barry, F. Dalou and J. Pommier.

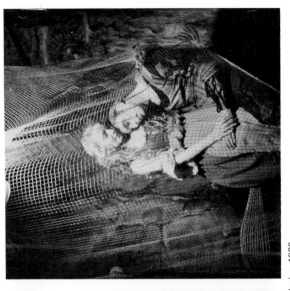

8. The set by Tchelitchew for *Ondine*, Théâtre de L'Athénée, 1939.

9. Madeleine Ozeray and Louis Jouvet in *Ondine*, 1939.

10. Louis Jouvet in *La Folle de Chaillot*, Théâtre de L'Athénée, 1945.

11. *La Folle de Chaillot*, 1945. M. Melinand, M. Moreno, Leo Lapara.

12. Georges Pitoëff in *Le Voyageur sans bagage*. Théâtre des Mathurins, February 1937.

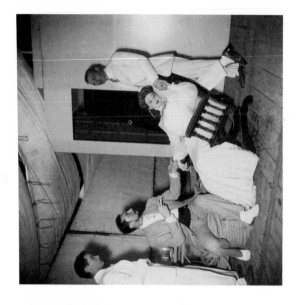

13. *Le Voyageur sans bagage*, 1937.

14. *Le Partage de Midi*, Théâtre Marigny, 1948. Jean-Louis Barrault, Pierre Brasseur, Edwige Feuillère, Jacques Dacqmine.

a comedy because of the puns, jokes, and innuendoes? Or a tragedy, since two people died? They questioned the meaning of the personification of Death, the use of unorthodox objects, the dehumanisation and ambiguous nature of the protagonists, the symbols and the sense of magic and mystery which pervaded the entire atmosphere.[2]

The sets, created by Jean-Victor Hugo, followed to a great extent Cocteau's own indications published in the first edition of his one-act and thirteen-scene play. *Orpheus* opens on a modern living room on an April day. The stage is brilliantly lit, the blueness of the sky is visible through the large windows. But there is something 'mysterious' about Orpheus' home and even the most routine and banal objects seem suspect: table, chairs, lamps, a large mirror. A *papier-maché* horse stands erect in a kind of circus box in a recess centre stage. His feet resemble those of a man. To the left, in another small recess adorned with laurel leaves, stands an empty pedestal.

A contemporary Orpheus and Eurydice are talking. Orpheus is dressed in a Chanel tennis outfit; his wife appears in a golfer's costume also created by that internationally famous dress designer. From the very outset, we learn that the Orpheus-Eurydice menage is not all that it was in antiquity. Orpheus loves the sun; Eurydice, the moon. They are opposites.

Eurydice is a grasping wife, jealous of Orpheus's love for poetry and his 'peculiar' attachment to a horse who serves as his muse. It is this animal which is going to reveal the sentence 'Madame Eurydice will return from Hades', that he hopes to immortalise in verse to be submitted to a poetry contest in Thrace. Orpheus accuses Eurydice of annoying him: 'Go into your room or keep quiet', he tells her in no uncertain terms, his voice controlled but strong and definite. He blames her for nagging him, for smashing windows just to attract the attention of the glazier, Heurtebise. He leaves the apartment in a huff, but before doing so (and to continue the pattern his wife has set), he smashes a window.

Heurtebise arrives. He is dressed in the pale blue overalls of a worker, has a dark scarf wrapped around his neck, and is wearing white espadrilles. He is sunburned and never once sets down his glazier's paraphernalia. Heurtebise, who is Eurydice's friend and confidant, has brought a lump of poisoned sugar to feed to Orpheus's horse; also an envelope from Aglaonice, Eurydice's best friend, a bacchant whom Orpheus despises. After placing a letter in the envelope given her by Heurtebise, Eurydice seals it and dies moments later from the poison placed on it by Aglaonice.

Death now enters the apartment through the large mirror on the wall, personified by a beautiful young woman wearing a brilliant rose-coloured evening dress and a coat. She strides across the stage, speaking in metallic tones to her two aides, Azael and Raphael, who are dressed in surgeons' uniforms. Before beginning her important work, Death removes her coat and one of her aides helps her don her white surgical gown; then she puts on her rubber gloves. She gives the horse the poisoned sugar, performs a series of rituals, then exits, forgetting her rubber gloves.

Orpheus and Heurtebise re-enter. When Orpheus learns that Eurydice has died, he is disconsolate, until Heurtebise shows him how to penetrate the land of Hades so he can join her. Orpheus puts on the rubber gloves Death left behind, steps into the mirror, then into Hades, 'Mirrors are the doors through which Death comes and goes'. Moments later, Orpheus returns with Eurydice. Death has granted her permission to remain on earth so long as Orpheus does not look at her. No sooner does she return, however, than their spats begin again. Orpheus inadvertently looks at her. She dies. Orpheus, seemingly unmoved, opens a letter left by the postman during his absence. It advises him to leave immediately; the bacchantes are coming in force and they are furious because they consider the poem he submitted to their contest a mockery. Orpheus, however, wants to resist the bacchantes and defend his ideas. He goes out onto the balcony to speak, is stoned, and is then torn to pieces. His head appears onstage, after which it disappears. In the last scene Eurydice and Orpheus, led by Heurtebise, are reborn in a kind of paradise. They go to their new house, having forgotten their past existences.

Cocteau was fascinated by the basic struggle between two forces in the universe, the solar (male) and the lunar (female) principles in religious worship. Aglaonice, a representative of the latter, was a sorceress and leader of the bacchantes. She was determined to draw Eurydice into her group in order to strengthen the dark cult of Hecate, which she represented. In Cocteau's play, Orpheus, in a moment of spite and anger, tells Eurydice to go back to the bacchantes since she likes their ways. Indeed, Eurydice resembles them: she is aggressive and possessive. Instead of the sensitive and retiring girl of Greek tradition, Parisian audiences were presented to a devouring and instinctual force of nature. Eurydice unable to fathom poetry, jealous and distrustful of her husband's interest in art, as symbolised by the horse's head, is a harrowing termagant à la Albee. Orpheus, the gentle poet, the male and spiritual counterpart of Eurydice and the Bacchantes, *vagina dentata* types, could not possibly escape from the clutches of these horrendous women, except in Cocteau's fairy-tale end, when Orpheus and Eurydice are reborn.

For Cocteau, Orpheus is also the modern poet in search of inspiration. Both priest and man, as was the legendary father of poetry and music, he must devote *all* his efforts and attention to his art, which is his religion. His marriage fatally diverts his 'fire' (energy) and his wife is jealous of his horse, Pegasus, who gives him some of his best ideas. Orpheus's trust and need for his horse increased as his own life became more and more unbearable. Let us not forget that Cocteau's Pegasus is not the fiery steed of antiquity, that powerful and gorgeously muscular animal. It has been reduced by the dramatist to a horse with human feet, placed in a circus box. Such a conception of poetic inspiration indicates a humorous and satiric intent, also a word of counsel. Inspiration can frequently play tricks on an unsuspecting poet; discernment and judgment, therefore, must always accompany any creative effort. The naive Orpheus lacks this discrimination and accepts at face value the dictates of his horse; he considers 'Madame Eurydice will return from Hades' to be a truly great line of verse.

Heurtebise, the glazier, was a guardian angel: a neuter force. He is the unwitting messenger of the evil bacchantes, the plaything of superior forces, and the inadvertent killer of Eurydice. But this winged angel is also a good power; it is he who discloses to Orpheus the means of passage from one world to the next; he also leads Orpheus and Eurydice to their new home, to paradise, in the last scene. He is a *deus ex machina*, a presence without whom the drama could never unfold.

The theme of death is also of great import in Cocteau's play. For the ancients, death was an initiation which each person must experience before passing into another realm of existence and undergoing rebirth. Cocteau considers life a temporary state; a passageway toward another realm. To pass from one state to the next, however, requires the completion of certain ordeals. That Death takes the form of a woman is plausible since woman is a procreating power and it is through Death that rebirth can occur. Cocteau's figure wears rubber gloves and operates with her two aides under strictly hygienic conditions. She is thus a twentieth-century figure. When she asks for her gloves, the audience understands the symbolism involved: she wants to prevent any contamination through contact with the world of mortals or matter. The rituals enacted by Death and her two aides undoubtedly have ironic overtones.

Theatrically, *Orpheus* is an exciting work. 'Even familiar objects,' Cocteau suggested in his preface to the play, have 'something suspicious about them.' They become ritualistic symbols, virtual protagonists. Divested of their customary functions, these entities (doors, mirrors, gloves, glass) acquire new and startling meanings. When worn by Death, rubber gloves gave audiences the impression of witnessing an actual operation; later, however, they seemed to turn into religious talismans endowed with the power to ensure safe passage from one world to the next. Mirrors likewise assume different functions. Habitually, they reflect a person's image, permitting one to indulge his or her narcissistic bent. In Cocteau's play, the mirror becomes an instrument by which one sees Death at work daily, 'You only have to watch yourself your whole life in a mirror and you'll see Death at work like bees in a glass hive'. In this mirror, humanity faces its own ageing and decaying self, as does Dorian Gray in the painting.

Cocteau introduced yet another interesting technique to his drama, mentioned briefly before: he purposefully broke audience-actor empathy. After Orpheus's death, for example, his head remained onstage. The audience was shocked and became even more so when the head began to talk and revealed its identity, declaring itself to be Jean Cocteau and giving its address. The destruction of the theatrical illusion served to reinforce it still further. The audience's identification went beyond the play's characters to the author himself. The spectators had become the dramatist's accomplice and were permitted to share in his secrets and his jokes. They were participating members of an arcane club.

Pitoëff's production of *Orpheus* was looked upon as both poetic and intelligent, pointing up the play's lyrical, emotional, and sensual qualities. His mise-en-scène underscored the magical and mythical dimensions of the multifaceted dialogue. As Orpheus, Georges Pitoëff played with verve and sensitivity, humour and a bent for the acidulous. His sharp and clipped vocal tones, his speedy or at times relatively slack verbal pace, both amused and disoriented viewers. Ludmilla Pitoëff brought out Eurydice's 'touching candor' in her portrayal, that of a *bourgeoise*. Heurtebise, portrayed by Marcel Herrand, discreet, serious, and tender in his ways, was so sprightly that he seemed to fly over the stage, emphasising in this manner the *heavenly* aspects of his personality. Particularly intriguing was the time when he climbed onto a chair to fix a window and Orpheus inadvertently came along and removed the chair. Heurtebise did not fall to the ground, but remained suspended in mid-air much to the astonishment of the audience. Death, incarnated by Mireille Havet, succeeded in implanting both delight and terror in the hearts of onlookers as she traversed 'those mysterious waters' through the mirror – equally at home in Hades or on earth. Elegant and sure of herself, she managed in the most dexterous way to blend theatre with the finest music-hall antics. She was truly an elegant transpersonal feminine image.[3]

8
Jean Giraudoux
(1882—1944)

Jean Giraudoux's plays in general, and *Ondine* and *The Madwoman of Chaillot* in particular, are mythical in dimension; universal in scope. Implicit in his works is the nobility and depth of Greek theatre; the structure, imagistic vocabulary, and rhythmic pace of French classical drama. Theatre, for Giraudoux had a historical and social mission: it was an educational device capable of enhancing the leisure hours of the working population; of encouraging people to think about spiritual as well as existential matters.

Myth, considered the narration of a primordial experience, fascinated Giraudoux. His *Amphitryon 38* (1929), the thirty-eighth version of the ancient story, tells of the seduction of the beautiful Alcmena by Jupiter when he assumes the form of her husband, the Theban general Amphitryon. *Intermezzo* (1933) dramatises a rite of passage: the transformation of the adolescent young girl, to the state of married woman and future mother. That war is an illusion which lulls people into believing that suffering and pain can be alleviated, is the theme of *Tiger at the Gates* (*La Guerre de Troie n'aura pas lieu* (1935). In *Electra* (1937), audiences witness the reworking of a great vengeance: Electra and her brother, Orestes, kill their mother, Clytemnestra, and her lover, Aegisthus, for having murdered Agamemnon, their father. Giraudoux was also drawn to Biblical stories, namely *Judith* (1931), which revolved around humankind's attempt to deny or defy an omnipotent destiny. The *Supplement to Cook's Voyage* (1935), praises the free and easy life in the South Seas prior to the introduction, by Christian missionaries, of 'civilisation', with its destructive concept of 'sin' and the notion that the body is 'evil'. Giraudoux's *Ondine* (1939) was inspired to a great extent by the work of the German nineteenth-century writer of fairy tales Baron Friedrich de La Motte-Fouqué (1777–1843). Society, with its evildoers and its good citizens, fired Giraudoux's imagination in the creation of *The Madwoman of Chaillot* (1945).

Giraudoux was born in Bellac in the Limousin, an area which he loved and in which he situated some of his novels and plays. After completing his *baccalauréat* at the Lycée of Châteauroux (1900), he entered the Lycée Lakanal in Paris, then studied at the famed Ecole Normale Supérieure. It was at this time that he took courses with Charles Andler, a well-known German professor at the Sorbonne, and developed a passion for nineteenth-century romantic Germany. In 1905 Giraudoux went to Munich to study; two years later he attended Harvard University as an exchange student. In 1910 he passed the French foreign service examination and began a longtime governmental career.

The meeting of Giraudoux with the well known director Louis Jouvet in 1927 was destined to be of great moment to both of them. It was under Jouvet's guidance that Giraudoux learned to write for the theatre. Jouvet taught him how to whittle down his narrative, how to underscore salient traits in a protagonist, how to develop tension, how to point up dialogue, tighten loose ends, and omit whatever did not contribute to the action or the development of character. Giraudoux rewrote *Siegfried* (1928) seven times. Most important, Jouvet made Giraudoux feel spiritually at home in the theatre, and under his guidance he became a notable playwright. But Jouvet, in turn, owed a great deal to Giraudoux. It was in his plays that Jouvet found the most suitable outlet for his talents, and with the introduction of Giraudoux's completely new and innovative style of playwriting, Jouvet reached his peak in French theatre.[1]

'Ondine' (1939)

Ondine opened on 4 May, 1939.[2] The decor, created by the noted artist Pavel Tchelitchew, drew accolades from an excited audience. Though the sets were simple, featuring a fisherman's cabin in the heart of the forest and near a lake, there was something disquieting about them. They strayed from reality and ushered in a dream atmosphere. The cabin's interior, draped with fish nets which hung gracefully from the heavy, hand-hewn beams, was both real and mysterious. The rough table placed in the centre of the stage and the stools around it were possessed, so it seemed, by some magical powers. As for the rainstorm in process, it made the dimming of the lights appropriate, while also encouraging strange and outerworldly feelings and thoughts to come to the fore.[3] As the play begins, Auguste and Eugénie, are talking about their adopted daughter, Ondine. They are concerned because she went out a long time ago and has not yet returned. She is not even fifteen and so innocent and naive – not like other children of her age. A knock is suddenly heard at the door. A knight-errant appears amid a clap of thunder; the shutters of the cabin bang furiously. He is in full armour and introduces himself as he clicks his heels: he is Ritter Hans von Wittenstein zu Wittenstein (portrayed by Louis Jouvet). He has been wandering, we learn, through the deep forest for many days and is thankful to have found a place where he can warm himself, eat, and feed his horse. He also tells the couple that he is engaged to the most perfect of women at court, Bertha. She has asked him to prove his worth before agreeing to their nuptials by spending a month in the forest (Jouvet's voice, which stayed on one note during his speech, emphasising each syllable rhythmically and sonorously, was reminiscent of ancient litanies or Gregorian chants and injected a mythical and eternal quality to the scene).

During the conversation, the cabin is suddenly flooded with light. A beautiful girl with long blond tresses is seen standing in the doorway: Ondine (portrayed by Madeleine Ozeray). Her ethereal and legendary side is underscored by the stage lighting, which veers from darkness to brilliant illumination. When she sees the knight-errant, she exclaims, 'How beautiful you are!'

Her sincerity and charm are dazzling; she is a 'miracle of youth'[4], a dream image. Auguste, however, rebukes her for her brazenness, but she repeats her comment in all sincerity. Embarrassed by Ondine's outspoken remark, the old couple explain that she lives with them; that they found her at the edge of the lake as a baby and brought her up in place of their own daughter, who vanished under mysterious circumstances when she was six months old.

Jean Giraudoux

Ondine is a water-sprite, a creature of the sea associated with siren myths found in medieval bestiaries as well as in the works of Homer, Aristotle, Pliny, and Ovid. Ondines incarnate the instinctual realm rather than the rational domain; they are universal and eternal, as Ondine herself says in the play: 'I was born centuries ago. And I shall never die.' Water-sprites, sirens, Loreleis, Melusines, and the like are archetypal and represent, psychologically speaking, inferior feminine forces, half-women and half-fish, they can neither satisfy men nor be satisfied by them. They are able to communicate with the animal world as well as with the spiritual realm; they can remain dry in the rain and see in total darkness; they entice men to enter the most primitive levels of existence, leading inevitably to self-destruction.

In that Ondine lives in perfect communion with nature, she has not learned, nor will she be able to learn, to be objective, to adapt to society, to utter the artifices required by town and castle life. On the contrary, she is *natural*: naive, sincere, filled with the beauty of the young, who look upon the world with openness and love. When she first sees Hans, so tall and handsome, she falls in love with him instantly, 'I knew there must be some reason for being a girl. The reason is that men are so beautiful.'

Ondine is volatile. Her mood suddenly changes when Eugénie, in keeping with the knight's wishes, brings him a blue trout to eat. Just as he is about to put it in his mouth, Ondine, who sees what has been done to an innocent creature – a member of her fish family – takes the entire dish and throws it out of the window. Eugénie apologises for Ondine's behaviour. Hans who has already fallen under the water-sprite's spell, asks only moments later for her hand in marriage. As for Ondine, she wants to enter the human sphere, to love and be loved. She is unaware, however, of the dangers awaiting the trustful, the innocent, in a world of hypocrisy, jealousy, and lust.

Before departing, Ondine speaks to her relative the king of the Ondines. He warns her not to follow her knight to court. She will be hurt and will learn the meaning of pain and suffering. No matter, she answers, she has made up her mind to return with Hans to court. If he deceives her, the king of the Ondines tells her, he will die. This is the rule of their world. Ondine is so much in love, so naive in the ways of humanity, that she does not even understand the meaning of what the king said.

Both Ondine and Hans, each emerging from opposite sides of worldly existence, had to encounter each other in a kind of rite of passage. Hans had to go through the *forest* experience, which meant returning to a primitive sphere that would give him the possibility of evolving in life. In court, he had met only the most superficial of people, who had cut him off from his world of feeling and sensation: the mainstream of life. His engagement to Bertha, and the constricted etiquette and hypocrisy of the court, had forced him to follow the mores and fashions of others, never being himself, never living authentically. He had reached a condition of stasis which had to be transcended. To withdraw to the forest meant to indwell, to sink into himself, to interiorise his energies, which were otherwise being diffused by coping with external problems. It is at this juncture that he meets Ondine, an archetypal figure. It is she who places Hans in contact with a sphere of being – nature – which until now he has neglected or rejected, or of which he has been unaware.

Act II takes Hans and his bride (he has just married Ondine) to the great hall of the court. The sets are spectacular in colour and design. Tchelitchew created the impression of immensity and fantasy through perspective:

by means of evenly spaced and alternating black and white marble columns. The white alabaster balustrade on either side of the stage was lighted from within. In the centre of the throne room were placed three chairs made of carved white coral. When the court officials walked onstage in their black, grey, white, green, and red costumes, with their white plumes and fancy laces, the extravagant daubs of colour lent a magical quality to the entire picture.

Preparations are being made for the arrival of the just-married couple. The royal chamberlain and the superintendent of the royal theatre are in the process of deciding on the proper entertainment for the guests. The king of the Ondines is also at court, unknown to all because he is disguised as the 'Illusionist'. He knows magic and can create any effect he wants in the most exciting of ways. The illusionist will play the role of fate, since he has the power to see into the future, which he intends to make known to the newlyweds. It is at this point that Ondine's problems will start, that her marriage will begin to disintegrate. The king, queen, and Bertha, as well as the other court officials, consider Ondine a usurper, a stranger who seduced Hans, winning his love away from his real bride, Bertha. Ondine's charm and sincerity fail to touch those she meets; instead she repels and infuriates them, and she begins to be despised. Hans is embarrassed by her statements and ways; also by the fact that she neither reads nor writes, nor does she dance. When Bertha asks Hans what Ondine does do, he replies, simply, 'She swims. Occasionally.'

Ondine's kingdom is the sea. Her frankness and her 'transparence' are unpleasant at court, where hypocrisy reigns. The Chamberlain considers her 'mad', as does Bertha. She cannot learn etiquette nor does she know how to behave socially and be polite, that is, lie or keep silent. The queen, who understands the beauty of Ondine's vision of the world and realises the impossibility of ever harmonising the natural with the artificial, counsels her to leave her husband: he does not understand her world which is peopled with birds, animals, and fish.

Water, which plays such a vital role in *Ondine* symbolises the source of life, activity, and potentiality. Psychologically, it stands for the unconscious, as does the forest, a sphere which nourishes an arid existential condition. To immerse oneself in water is to regress to a preformal state and in this way to start anew – to be reborn. When relationships go askew, they need renewal and rejuvenation. So Hans and Ondine, who are both unbalanced in their own ways, must replenish their one-sided natures: he through his forest experience, she through the fluid waters of the unconscious.

In Act III we learn that Ondine cannot fit into the court system and comes into overt conflict with Bertha. The Illusionist does rescue her from some difficult moments, however, when he reveals to everyone that Bertha is really the lost daughter of Auguste and Eugenie, and consequently must leave the court. Hans has died because he deceived Ondine. She, however, remembers nothing and returns to the realm of the sea, but on the way, she sees a man lying on a marble slab and questions his identity, 'Why is this handsome young man lying here? Who is he?' The king of the Ondines tells her that his name is Hans. 'Can he be brought back to life again?' she questions. No, is the answer. 'What a pity!' she reflects. 'How I should have loved him.'

Two worlds are juxtaposed in *Ondine*: the natural and the artificial, the primitive and the civilised, beauty and ugliness; the 'dark angel', Bertha, and the force of light, Ondine. In the Jouvet production these dual worlds were made all the more incompatible by the quality of the sets and lighting and the acting techniques of the performers.

Reviews of the play were mixed. All the critics praised Tchelitchew's sets for their exciting colours, their poetry, and their dreamlike quality. Sauguet's music was lauded for its lively cadences, its harsh and strident notes, which replicated Giraudoux's own rhythms and sonorities; its reinforcement of the atmosphere of myth and magic. Ozeray was commended for her lithe and lively interpretation, the strange beauty she succeeded in incorporating into her role, the richness of her tonal pitches, and the delicacy and savor of her charm. She knew most perfectly how to portray this creature of the sea and make her captivating and seductive, but in the most 'adorable' and 'fantastic' of ways. She was the image of delight, sensitivity, outspokenness, as she paraded about in circles and arabesques on stage.

Jouvet also captivated audiences. When he first appeared onstage, his voice was rude and warlike, revealing his lack of delicacy and sensibility. He was not a fundamentally cruel fellow but was unaware of the more sensitive things in life. He loved war for the opportunities it offered him. After falling in love with Ondine, however, his character slowly underwent a change, as if influenced by some tender magical force. He became gentle, speaking in *sotto voce* tones. A critic wrote, 'The voice rarely departs from a pivotal note, within the limits of a third. The syllables are of equal duration.' Jouvet's measured ways, the tender way he conveyed his simple passion for Ondine (as opposed to his sensual attraction for Bertha), emphasised the dichotomy in his heart, the conflict he was unable to resolve, between purity and the hypocrisy inherent in court life.[5]

Although the critics considered the second act overly long, awkward, laboured, drowned in extraneous incidents and detail which neither enhanced the plot nor the actors' play, Jouvet's production of *Ondine* was memorable. 'The tragic excludes neither gaiety nor laughter,' Giraudoux had written. As a tragedy, *Ondine* is a composite of both.[6]

'The Madwoman of Chaillot' (1942)

The Madwoman of Chaillot is also mythical in focus. It deals with the struggle waged by light against darkness, by honourable preservers against unscrupulous exploiters, by those who would build a society against others who would destroy it.

The Madwoman of Chaillot was produced under difficult conditions. Outside of the lack of funds prevailing after the German occupation during World War II, it was the first time that Giraudoux was not present to help Jouvet stage one of his works. Jouvet had been in Rio de Janeiro when Giraudoux sent him his play, in 1942. On the cover of the manuscript he had written prophetically, '*The Madwoman of Chaillot* was performed for the first time on 17 October, 1945, on the stage of the Athénée Theatre by Louis Jouvet.' Giraudoux died on 31 January, 1944. The curtains opened on Jouvet's production two months and two days after the date predicted: 19 December, 1945.[7]

Giraudoux's two-act play takes place in Paris in the early 1900s in front of the Cafe Chez Francis on Alma Place in the Chaillot district. The sets, created by the painter Christian Bérard, were wistful and poetic. The cafe stood in the centre of the stage, and above it was an apartment house, three stories high with four rows of windows, each laced with a filigree railing. Only one window was open. For some inexplicable reason, the building gave the impression of being suspended from the sky, and this suffused a spirit of unreality into the surroundings. Chairs and tables stood under the canopy and to the right was some greenery. The lighting was bright; the season was spring.

Since Giraudoux divides society into two classes – the 'good' and 'mad' people versus the 'evil' ones – both groups are present onstage and congregate in front of Chez Francis. The barons, presidents, financiers, and capitalists represent the negative elements. They are the ones who want to create a cartel and take the oil which, they have been told, exists underneath the cafe. To acquire this oil necessitates the destruction of the neighbourhood, which attracts so many by its charm. The other group, which includes the Madwoman of Chaillot, the ragpicker, the dishwasher, the sewerman, and the flower girl, will try to rectify a wrong by controlling the forces that would divest the world of joy and pleasure.

The role of the Madwoman of Chaillot is unique in theatre. Marguerite Moréno, who played this part, was dressed in the most outlandish ways. On top of her tremendous hat trimmed with flounces was perched a pigeon carrying a letter in its beak. Her dress was bedecked with false pearls, laces, and many other incredible trinkets. Her face was old and heavily made up with flour; her eyes were circled with charcoal. The effect of her clownlike face and the many brilliant reds, greens, yellows, and purples on her dress was kaleidoscopic.

As the Madwoman of Chaillot and her friends, the simple folk of Paris, walked out onstage on the opening night to face the gangsters and profiteers who sought to take over the neighbourhood, the city, and the world, the audience was thrilled. Eccentric, absurd, or even crazy, each of the Madwoman's friends, in his or her own way, understood the dangers involved, the possibility of ending life as they all knew it.

The ragpicker, played by Jouvet, explains the situation, 'There's been an invasion, Countess,' he says to the Madwoman of Chaillot. 'The usurpers who seek to possess everything' – 'pimps,' as they are called – were identified with the forces of the German occupation. 'In the old days,' the ragpicker continues, 'the people one met in the street were like us, perhaps better-dressed or dirtier, but pleasant.' He warns those present that they must act and struggle as the head of their neighbourhood, the head of their government, to prevent further encroachment by evil forces.

When Jouvet, portraying the ragpicker, walked out onstage with trepidation, a hush filled the house as the audience watched him about to speak his first lines. Tenderly and firmly he began, shoulders slightly hunched, his glance turned down in a constant search for cast-away cigarette butts, his nostrils sniffing the smell (perfume to him) of ashtrays. The spectators were slowly caught up in the grip of the play and Jouvet felt the rising tension in the theatre. He knew at this moment that he had captured their attention; that they were his. He breathed more easily as the play pursued its course.

A sentimental situation is implicit in all of Giraudoux's plays, and *The Madwoman of Chaillot* is no exception. A gentle, sweet, and naive dishwasher, Irma, and her young and equally innocent boyfriend, Pierre, have a serious problem that must be ironed out. Pierre has committed a minor crime: he has written a check without having sufficient funds in the bank and is being blackmailed by the villainous usurpers, who want to force him to participate in their dishonest deals. Pierre, however, whose integrity is unimpeachable, would rather die than yield to their nefarious plans. He tries to commit suicide, but is rescued in time and given a *raison d'être* to live by the Madwoman of Chaillot.

136

Jean Giraudoux

It is the Madwoman of Chaillot who, having learned about the schemes of the profiteers to destroy a way of life, thinks of a plan to save the neighbourhood, the people, and society in general. She invites some of her friends to a meeting in her apartment: the Madwoman of Saint-Sulpice (played by Raymone), the Madwoman of the Concorde (played by Lucienne Bogaert), the Madwoman of Passy (played by Marguerite Mayane), and all the young folks.

Act II has a different quality to it. It takes place in a shabby basement apartment in Chaillot Street. The apartment communicates through a trap door with the sewers of Paris, and the Madwoman of Chaillot's friends enter her domain through this secret passageway. When Bérard designed the sets for this act, he realised he would have to avoid the obvious and never fall into the commonplace. His setting was semi-fantastic. The stage was circular: the lighting and sets were shadowy and phantomesque. The curtain went up on an immense, leprous-looking room filled with broken pieces of furniture and bric-a-brac of all sorts: a rocking chair draped in black velvet, splintered chandeliers resembling transparent stalactites, monstrous plants, a tabouret, a screen, several hangings all awry, and a turquoise clothes horse. The last lending a more luxurious note in sharp contract with the decaying green mould on the walls. The lighting was so manipulated as to produce soft reflections on the mouldy walls, which at times made them seem draped in silk. In the centre of this tremendous cellar, was a huge bed, with a red canopy suspended by a wire from the ceiling. In the rear, rather close to the ceiling, there were two small barred windows. In this cellar, the Madwoman of Chaillot, dressed in a purplish-red velvet dressing gown, received the ladies of her court. The Madwoman of Passy was dressed in white from the tips of her plumes to her high-laced boots. The Madwoman of

137

Saint-Sulpice was decked out in black. The Madwoman of the Concorde, sitting in uncertain balance on an armchair, nervously fingered her tawdry finery, the laces and silks which had once, long ago, been *haute couture*. The rest of the characters appeared in less striking tones: whites, browns, blacks, tans, ochres.

A mock trial is called for by the Madwoman of Chaillot. Each person, she states, must enact the role of a profiteer, a financial baron. We learn that these evil people have already taken over the castles of the Loire as their personal residences, and other areas as well. The ragpicker takes up the defense of the profiteers before what he terms his 'élite and elegant public'. Irony is implicit in each of his words, which he speaks out clearly and slowly, sustaining all the colour and emotion inherent in the text. He tells those seated in judgment how he made his money, how he traded stock, bought businesses. He really hates money, he says, but he is stuck with it, ashamed because it seems to follow him wherever he is and whatever he does. He tries to win the sympathy of the court by telling them how he 'sends to Java for flowers' and how he cannot seem to get rid of his gold, his diamonds. He even threw some diamonds into the Seine – which were returned to him. What is his crime?

Of course the court finds the capitalist guilty, and the Madwoman of Chaillot will put through her plan. She invites the profiteers to her basement apartment, promising them they can examine the earth beneath her cellar to see if there is really oil there. She thanks the ragpicker for the impartiality of his speech and demands full power to carry out her plan from all those present.

The president, prospectors, and advertisers all enter and file past, carrying a gold brick and papers giving them the power to place the Madwoman of Chaillot in an insane asylum and keep the oil money for themselves. Meanwhile,

Irma, the dish-washer, gives each of them a glass of water tasting of petrol, which fills them with incredible excitement at the thought of all the money they will make once they rid themselves of this Madwoman and take over her apartment. The Madwoman invites them to descend into a subcellar, through her trapdoor, so as to better examine the soil beneath. Little do they know that this is a ruse. Once they, and three women who also arrive on the scene, drawn to the lucre to be made, are out of sight, the trap door is shut and sealed. There is no escape for the evil ones now.

Critics were unanimous in their praise: they called *The Madwoman of Chaillot* a 'truly great play' and alluded 'to a rare moment in the theatre'; to a 'sparkling evening', to 'pure poetry', to 'an innovative work'. Nor was there a gesture which was out of place in the entire mise-en-scène. Each actor played his or her part as it should be: with spontaneity yet dignity, with a lifelike quality which gave it a natural and realistic touch, as though the Madwoman of Chaillot and her cronies really existed. The succession of silhouettes, be they good or evil, were arresting. Characteristically, every detail had been planned in the most minute way by Jouvet prior to the opening. Frequently, particularly in Act II, the rhythmical interchanges between the characters took on a balletlike quality, as though everything was moving, all was connected and interlinked: good and evil. *The Madwoman of Chaillot* was 'disarming' – a 'triumph'.[8]

Giraudoux has not ceased to enchant his audiences, young and old. The sumptuousness of his language, its musicality and rhythmic qualities, its feeling tones, distilled in subdued and subtle ways into his situations and relationships, answer a need in the theatregoer. He had that rare gift of being able to communicate directly with the spectators because, for him, the theatre was 'not a theorem, but a spectacle; not a lesson, but a filter.'[9]

9
Jean Anouilh
(1910—   )

Theatre 'must create by every artifice possible something truer than truth,' wrote Jean Anouilh.[1] He has succeeded admirably in achieving his goal in *The Traveller Without Luggage* (1937), and in many other plays. The theatrical medium was a perfect vehicle for him to lay bare the soul of his protagonists, to probe those eternal questions of identity, integrity, and the dichotomy between the real and the unreal worlds. The techniques used by him to point up the ambiguities and contentions which lie at the heart of his works (coincidences, shock, improvisation, puns, jokes, the play within the play, a variety of images and symbols, masks, and other devices) also convey the mysteries of the heart and mind which haunt humankind. The multiple attitudes toward life which Anouilh delineates in his stage plays may seem harsh and brutal at times; nevertheless, they enrich the viewer and the reader by underscoring the indecisive nature of so many who seem to be immersed in an ever-alluring fantasy world. Derisive, fascinating, frustrating, his works are endowed with point and humour, with artistry; they glisten with urgency and meaning.

Anouilh divides his theatre into several categories, each reflecting a different outlook toward people and things, each mirroring the feelings of those who struggle against a society they consider to be built on compromise and deceit. Anouilh's universe is peopled by heroes and anti-heroes, the pure and the impure: those who express a need for love and romance, those who seek money and power. Caricatures also stalk the stage, motivated by base and selfish urges or guided by compassion, gentleness, and a deep feeling for humankind.

Anouilh labelled his first category of plays 'Black Plays', and they include *The Ermine* (1931), *Jezebel* (1932), *The Traveller Without Luggage* (1937), and others. These works are peopled with beings who cannot accept or face themselves, their past deeds in particular; who fail for the most part in their attempt to escape from the image they have of themselves and others. For them, society is sordid; it is the great corrupter of morals and is divested of any code of honour. Anouilh's 'Pink Plays', which include *The Thieves Carnival* (*Le Bal des voleurs*, 1932), *Rendez-vous at Senlis* (*Le Rendez-vous de Senlis*, 1937), and *Leocadia* (1939), are a bit less depressing. Escape into a world of multiple personalities is in the offing here; fantasies brought into existence through humorous and satiric circumstances and coincidences alleviate what could be a protracted sense of pathos. The 'Brilliant Plays' comprise *The Invitation to the Castle* (*L'Invitation au château*, 1947), and blend with felicity some of the techniques used in the 'Black' and 'Pink' plays. The 'Jarring Plays', such as *Becket* (1959), which delineates the precarious relationships between Henry Plantagenet and his prime minister, and others, reflect a pessimistic view of life. In Anouilh's dramas concerning legendary figures (*Eurydice*, 1941; *Antigone*, 1942; *Orestes*, 1945; *Medea*, 1946), he underscores the tragedy of an individual who attempts to modify the role which he is destined to play during his life on earth. As Medea tells her little son at the conclusion of the play, 'Hurry, hurry, little one, and you will finish your role, you'll be able to go back and enjoy yourself.'

'I have no biography,' Anouilh said vehemently when people attempted to find out some details concerning his life,' and I am delighted about this.'[2] He does admit, however, to having a *métier*: he 'makes acts' the way others construct chairs. We do know that Anouilh was born at Cérisole, a small town near Bordeaux; that he went to primary and secondary school in Paris; that he studied law for six months and served as secretary to Louis Jouvet at the Comédie des Champs-Elysées. Anouilh was so poor at the time that Jouvet lent him the sets for *Siegfried* to furnish his home after his marriage to the actress Monelle Valentin.

It was Giraudoux, perhaps more than any other writer, who influenced Anouilh's style. As secretary to Jouvet, Anouilh was in a position to learn the intricacies of theatre and Giraudoux's playwriting methods and disciplines in particular. It was perhaps the older playwright's sense of poetry and fantasy, his humour and the depth of his portrayals, that most impressed Anouilh. From the works of Luigi Pirandello (1867–1936), including *Six Characters in Search of an Author*, Anouilh learned how to create suspense through evocative and anticipatory situations, whisperings, the introduction of mysterious and shadowy creatures, flashbacks, dreams, the play within the play. Pirandello's *As You Desire Me* dramatises the theme of amnesia, foreshadowing in some respects Anouilh's *The*

Traveller Without Luggage. The traditions of the Italian *commedia dell'arte* and of Molière's farcelike routines – especially their use of improvisation and stock characters to play out eternal types, and their variety of disguises and personalities, which lend amplitude to the stage creations – also made inroads into Anouilh's theatre.

Anouilh is very much a contemporary writer, and no play of his better than *The Traveller Without Luggage* expresses modern anguish, solitude, isolation, and perception of life's absurdity. If one is divested of faith and love is considered illusory and elusive, integrity a meaningless ideal, life becomes virtually intolerable. Should it be accepted or rejected? Or should one attempt to escape into another sphere of being?

'The Traveller Without Luggage' (1936)

When Georges Pitoëff, the director of *The Traveller Without Luggage*, first read Anouilh's play, he was so impressed with its depth, its technical mastery, and the authentic ring of the scenario that he visualised the entire work on the stage at that very moment, in his mind's eye.[3] Pitoëff's instinctual reaction was the correct one. Opening night, 16 February, 1937, at the Théâtre des Mathurins earned Anouilh his first theatrical success.[4]

The Traveller Without Luggage deals with an amnesia case, that of a war casualty, as had Giraudoux's *Siegfried*. While there were political ramifications written into Giraudoux's play (he hoped for a reconciliation between Germany and France), Anouilh's drama revolves around a protagonist's past and the problems posed by his reintegration into the present.

To enhance the pathos as well as the satiric, even comic, intent of the play, Darius Milhaud's incidental music emphasised its variety of moods, which ranged from mocking banter to lascivious, solemn, and highly tense moments. The rhythms, a composite of slow-paced and accelerated beats, underscored the protagonist's deeply set conflicts. When he was forced to relive an unpleasant incident in the past, the tones became macabre, heavy, and difficult to bear. When absurdity took over, at the conclusion, the musical language expressed this state of affairs with a tremolo from the orchestra, and the curtains came down on a medley of triumphant sounds. 'Each time the text requires a prolongation,' Pitoëff declared, 'music intervenes. . . . Not that music attempts to express the inexpressible', but it served the text, poignantly and profoundly.[5]

The Traveller Without Luggage opens in the living room of an opulent home in the French countryside. A meddlesome old woman, the Duchess Dupont-Dufort, is talking to the maître d'hôtel about a young officer, Gaston, who was found eighteen years ago, in 1918, near a prisoner-of-war train. Because he could not even remember his own name or anything about his past, he was taken to a psychiatric hospital and named Gaston. Now, six families (there were more at the outset, but for one reason or another, the others were eliminated) claim him as their long-lost son. Gaston is in the process of visiting each of these families, hoping, during the course of these meetings, that some person or object will restore some part of his memory. Gaston is expected at the Renaud's home soon after the curtains part. He, as the possible Jacques Renaud, will meet his brother, Georges, and his wife, Valentine, as well as his mother and the servants.

Pitoëff's production of Anouilh's play featured relatively sparse settings, a hallmark of this extraordinary director. He wanted to give *The Traveller Without Luggage* the impression of moral and psychological divestiture, despite the family's wealth and sense of class. More significant for Pitoëff than the stage properties were the feelings to be evoked in the portrayal of Gaston (Pitoëff himself took this role): the sense of someone being awakened to a world buried deeply within the dimly lit areas of the unconscious. Pitoëff stripped his Gaston, visually and emotionally, down to the essentials – to the bone. When he walked out onstage as Gaston, Pitoëff's lithe body, his large forehead, his piercing black eyes, conveyed feelings of the deep torment of not being able to recall one's past, to be without identity.

As Gaston enters the living room and is greeted ever so graciously by the duchess, a friend of the family, he appears detached. In no way is he disconcerted by her excessive and fanciful imagination, her rapid chatter, which make her appear ridiculous, but highly comical, reminiscent of those marvellous characters in Feydeau drawing room comedies. Gaston seems to be oblivious to the outside world. He merely walks about and looks at the paintings on the walls, not paying the slightest bit of attention to the duchess or to a solicitor who is also present. Like a child visiting a new house, swept up by the novelty of it all, he looks at everything wide-eyed, naively, intent upon learning and discovering the truth about himself. Yet, despite his outward complacency, the enigma of his past and the emotional uncertainty of a mysterious present weigh heavily upon him. The duchess, for her part, doesn't begin to understand the deeper meaning of his causal and offhand manner, his seeming indifference to a world which she is certain is his. Gaston's ascetic form moves about, observing intently; his expression changes ever so subtly, giving the impression of an untapped dimension which is there for the asking.

As he looks at the paintings and apparently enveloped in

a dream, he is meditating upon a life that could have been
had he never left this household. He certainly would have
been a father by now, he muses, and a smile crosses his face.
As this expository scene pursues its course, we learn that
Gaston had felt relaxed in the mental institution, comfortable in the little fantasy world he had created for himself.
From the moment the Renaud family, and the others, had
urged him to leave and discover his real home, a world into
which he could integrate himself, this secure existence had
come to an end. He had to 'find' a new *I* and put it on like an
old vest.

The duchess tells Gaston that he is just like Jacques: as
cold as marble and as unfeeling as stone. Little by little
Gaston learns that Jacques was far from pleasant. Nor is the
rest of the Renaud family worthy of admiration: Mme
Renaud is snobbish and class-conscious; Georges is passive, more interested in playing out the role of a rich
bourgeois than seeking purity of soul; his wife, Valentine,
we discover had been Jacques' mistress and is corrupt in all
ways.

Just as Gaston has examined the paintings in the living
room, thoughtfully and intently, so he now stops in front of
each member of the Renaud family and looks at them in
silence, powerfully, as if attempting to ferret out the
minutest of clues that would trigger his memory. When he
stands immobile in front of Valentine, the audience hears
her murmur almost imperceptibly, 'My darling. . .' Gaston, who knows nothing as yet of his former liaison with
her, is astonished. After completing his visual examination,
he throws up his arms in despair. He recalls nothing.

In the Second Tableau, worthy of a Feydeau or Labiche
bedroom farce, we see some of the servants peering
through a keyhole and commenting on what they see. As
they chat and gossip, they fill the gaps concerning Jacques'

adolescent years. From them we learn that Jacques was spoiled, selfish, jealous, malicious, and generally 'evil'. Not one pleasant characteristic is mentioned – nothing that could endear him to anyone.

Later, Gaston is shown around the bourgeois home, with its long and gloomy halls, its vestibules, its large staircase, hoping that some object or person will arouse some part of his past. But there is nothing that moves him in any way. He seems to be cut off from a past hidden in this house and from this family. The fantasy world he created for himself in the mental institution has taken over. It is beautiful and pure, and perhaps, unconsciously, he does not want to alter it or exchange it for a world of reality that is proving itself to be more and more insidious.

As Pitoëff/Gaston looked around the room, the mystery embedded in the past increased in intensity. The stage space was transformed into a kind of sacred sphere where revelations could come into being. The shadowy lighting effects increased this outerworldly impression, as if these illuminations were paving the way for the resurgence of spectres who would appear and disappear according to their own laws. Feelings of all types, including passion and passivity, love and hate, frustration and rage, lived out their prodigious existences in the fantasy world that Pitoëff conveyed each time he looked about in wonderment and bedazzlement. His control and distancing, his withdrawal into a secret inner realm, seemed to increase the tension of the hidden drama being lived out by each member of the family.

When Gaston finally learns that Jacques threw his best friend down the stairs for having tried to kiss his mistress, the maid Juliette, and that this fall caused his paralysis and death, he is overcome with revulsion. He is even more disgusted with Juliette, who tells him how proud she was of being worthy of his attention and of being the cause of a fight. It is also at this point that Gaston becomes aware that Jacques was indifferent to people and to life. He never questioned any of his acts; nor did he have any sense of morality. When Valentine, a perfidious coquette, tells Gaston that she was Jacques' mistress and loved him despite his character defects, and that her husband Georges accepted the situation for social and economic reasons, Gaston feels sickened by the thought that he might be Jacques. He is aghast when Valentine tells him she wants to pursue their relationship, reminding him that she visited him in the asylum, where they made love, though Gaston did not recognise her.

Pitoëff/Gaston winced each time he heard tell of another sordid escapade on Jacques' part; the restraint with which he enunciated his lines added greatly to the intensity of the scene. Gaston keeps questioning the family in a thoughtful and posed manner, as if his emotions are boxed in; only his eyes and facial expressions convey the depths of his anguish. A change in countenance and demeanour takes place when Gaston confronts his mother, a hard and dry woman, who also seeks to reclaim him. Prior to his departure for the war, it seems, he and his mother did not speak for over a year. They had a rift over a seamstress Jacques wanted to marry. Since Mme Renaud was very class-conscious, she would not hear of such a misalliance and refused her permission; was even unwilling to say goodbye to her son when he left for the army. She recounts her last conversation with him, when her son blurted out, 'I hate you'. So identified is Gaston with Jacques at this point, so shocked is he by his mother's cold indifference (she did not even kiss him before he went to the front), that an insurmountable barrier is created between them. There was never any mother-son rapport, he realises, because love was lacking, integrity was dormant, beauty of soul was an unknown quantity. For the first time, feeling erupts within Gaston. After a pause, he can no longer contain his rage; with eyes vacant, his thoughts elsewhere, as though he has regressed to a terrifying past, he blurts out, 'It's true, I hate you'.

His mother is horror-stricken. She doesn't know what has possessed him. Moments later, however, Gaston takes hold of himself and apologises. 'I am not Jacques Renaud,' he tells her strongly and emphatically. 'I know nothing about what he was' (III). He does admit to having had, just for a moment, a kind of lapse and again excuses himself for it. 'For a man without a memory, a whole past is just too heavy a proposition to shoulder all at once.'

The Traveller Without Luggage, a drama based upon interrogation, gains momentum with each succeeding scene, reaching full force as Jacques discovers the amount of evil he had once perpetrated; his thoughtlessness, his egotism. 'The bastard,' Gaston mutters under his breath, filled with disgust, his words reveberating throughout the theatre.

In the Fifth Tableau, we see Gaston as he is about to awaken in Jacques' bedroom. The duchess and the maître d'hôtel have placed all of his little stuffed animals around his bed, hoping in this way to arouse his memory. When Gaston awakens and discovers that one of his favourite pastimes had been killing birds and small animals, then having them stuffed, the impression of outer tranquillity which he has given until now grows increasingly shaky, revealing the trauma he now experiences.

When Valentine insists once again that they continue their relationship, Gaston finally decides to reject his past and all those who had peopled this world. To do so is impossible, Valentine tells him; to do away with a past is to

reject oneself. Only at this juncture does she tell him she is
the only one who can prove his true identity, that he is
Jacques: she had made a scar on his back with a pin when
she thought he had been unfaithful to her. Gaston replies,
still composed, 'I am probably the only man, it's true, to
whom destiny will have given the possibility of realising a
dream which everyone cherishes.'

Moments later, in one of the most dramatic and poignant
scenes of the play, audiences see two servants standing on a
stool peering through a transom, relaying what they
observe: Gaston is removing his clothes, then looking at
himself in a mirror and beginning to weep. What makes this
scene stand out so powerfully is that all sentiment has been
banished; the vulgarity and humorous innuendoes of the
servants' dialogue as they report the happenings, and the
matter-of-fact way they deal with pathos and deep pain,
stand out starkly.

Gaston, looking into the mirror for one long moment,
grabs an object on the table and smashes the glass; then he
sits on the bed and covers his face with his hands. In a kind
of *deus ex machina* ending, a young boy (played by
Ludmilla Pitoëff), dressed in an Eton suit, the only survivor
of an English branch of a family, arrives with his uncle, Mr.
Pickwick. They are looking for a missing nephew, and if
they do not find him the young lad will lose his inheritance.
Gaston decides to live in their beautiful home in Sussex.
There will be no memories to confront, since no one who
had known the missing nephew is still alive; no past will
have to be lived out.

Gaston returns to a past without, paradoxically, a past.
This rather forced ending underscores the impossibility of
coming to terms with a life that represents everything that is
distasteful to an individual. When Gaston forcibly rejects
his family and his world, he is in fact doing away with an

aspect of himself which he feels is not redeemable. During his eighteen years in the mental institution, he had created a *façon d'être*, a morality which he felt was beautiful and with which he could live comfortably. He cannot now, nor does he want to, create a third personality which would combine his evil characteristics with his ideal fantasy world, thereby integrating polarities.

Pitoëff's portrayal of Gaston's attempt to deal with a flawed personality was subdued and underplayed – bringing out, as he did, the pathos involved in his brief glimpses into past situations, which made him cringe, tremble physically. The precision of Pitoëff's speech, articulated in various rhythmic patterns and tonalities, and the crescendos to which it led, disclosed the power inherent in these secret recesses of his soul. Decanting his emotions with utmost restraint, Pitoëff gave the impression of containing, as best he could, a volcano on the verge of exploding.

'You cannot imagine what *you* and *The Traveller Without Luggage* have done for me,' Anouilh wrote to Pitoëff; 'you have both enriched and paralysed me.' Anouilh was moved by the poetry of the performance as well as its craftsmanship, which injected into his work the realism he had intended to convey. The critics were equally enthusiastic: they pointed up Pitoëff's discreet and sober mise-en-scène, which emphasised mounting feelings of panic as the protagonist discovered the distressing shadows peopling his inner world. Pitoëff's acting added considerably to the richness of the charcter: a surreal mood was injected into his portrayal, as though he were absorbed in another realm, blocked, meditative, preoccupied with some special considerations. The cast as a whole was singled out for praise: for the authenticity of their creations.[6]

Jean Anouilh

Anouilh's theatre is mythical. His characters or caricatures remain indelibly fixed in the mind of audiences and
readers alike as they parade their distorted, depersonal-
ised, and frequently degrading visions side-by-side with
their beautiful and ethereal outlooks on existence.
Although life for Anouilh's creatures is a masquerade, in
The Traveller Without Luggage, it may be made meaningful
no matter what the baggage one must drag along. Choice is
each person's weapon to fight off melancholia and distress.
One may make a *tabula rasa* of one's past, rectify injustices,
wipe the slate clean and start anew.

Tragedy and comedy comingle in Anouilh's theatre,
which deals so delightfully and poignantly with eternal
problems. The verve and brilliance of the dialogue, the brio
and poetry of the music, and the masterly mise-en-scène all
work together to create rare and exciting moments in
theatre.

10
Paul Claudel
(1868–1955)

Break of Noon, one of the great plays of the twentieth century, is archetypal in magnitude. It centres upon 'adultery' – a wife, a husband, and two lovers. It dramatises the struggle between 'the religious vocation and the call of the flesh'.[1] The flesh dominates. Every word in *Break of Noon* breathes with Dionysian fervour and jubilation. Yet counterforces follow each euphoric experience, shedding feelings of shame and guilt in their wake. The intensity of these clashing emotions – exquisite sensuality in pursuit of forbidden fruit, and terror engendered by belief in the damnation to follow – heightens the excitement and titillates the senses. Claudel's creatures are pagans clothed in Catholic vestments; they are hedonists yearning to be ascetics.

Claudel, born in the town of Villeneuve-sur-Fère-en Tardenois in the Aisne region, was fourteen when he and his family, all but the father, moved to Paris. In 1886 he discovered *The Illuminations* by Arthur Rimbaud. This slim volume of poems was to become a 'seminal' force in his life, because it opened up 'the supernatural world' to him. The year 1886 was also of extreme significance because it brought Claudel the answer to his metaphysical anguish. During the Christmas mass at Notre Dame Cathedral in Paris, he was so shaken by the experience of divinity that he was 'converted' to the faith of his fathers. By 1900, Claudel had decided to go on a retreat to Solesmes, then enter the Benedictine monastery of Ligugé and become a monk. His religious vocation was short-lived because his spiritual director believed the poet unsuited for monastic life. Claudel returned to the world.

For Claudel, drama seemed the most expressive of creative forms. It allowed him to quell antagonisms breeding within him and to expel these in palpable creatures. In *Golden Head (Tête d'Or*, 1889) the protagonist (who gives the play its title) was a conqueror, a rebellious, active being who rejected the status quo, fomented divisiveness, and aroused fresh ideas and ideals. *The City (La Ville*, 1890) was set in the Sodom and Gomorrah atmosphere in which Claudel felt 'plunged' at the time. *The Tidings Brought to Mary (L'Annonce faite à Marie*, 1910–11), was a religious mystery in which the spirit of sacrifice becomes the dominant theme.

Claudel entered the foreign service and left for China, where he stayed from 1895 to 1900. A year after his return to France, he was sent back to China (1901), where he remained until 1905. The political situation in China at this time was difficult and dangerous because of the Boxer Rebellion, which had begun in 1900. The Boxers, a secret society bent upon killing or deporting all foreigners, whom they felt had virtually dismembered their land, were very active and had laid siege to Peking. The uprising was suppressed by joint European action.

It was on the *Ernest-Simons*, the ship returning Claudel

to China, that he met the beautiful Polish blond, Rose Vetch, wife and mother. His passion for her was great and was reciprocated. Despite the commandments of his religion and the fact that only months prior to his traumatic love affair he had wanted to become a monk, his liaison, which included the birth of a child, lasted for several years. Whatever the reason for his 'breakup', he expressed his grief most powerfully in his great dramatic work *Break of Noon*, which he alluded to as a 'deliverance', and which he wrote 'with his blood', he said.[2] So personal, so traumatic a drama was it that he refused to allow it to be staged 'officially' until 1948, when Jean-Louis Barrault was awarded this singular honour. *The Satin Slipper* (*Le Soulier de Satin*, 1919–24) concludes the cycle of Claudel's plays about Rose. This second work, in which the notions of denial, sublimation, and the joy of encountering and sacrificing one's passion are uppermost, is overly intellectual in construction. What is lacking in this complex drama is sincerity. Structure is all-important. Theology in its syllogistic array is its focal point.

Claudel's theatre is sensual and erotic. His poetics, based on powerful imagery, rhythmic and breathing techniques, stylised gestures, religiously oriented themes, and intensely cruel love episodes, is, technically speaking, adventuresome. By combining the eurythmics of Emile Jacques Dalcroze, the film projection techniques of Erwin Piscator, and by using the vast scenic spaces in spectacularly new ways, as Max Reinhardt had suggested, Claudel succeeded in injecting a cosmic dimension into his plays.

Claudel was a strong believer in eurythmics: a technique which coordinates bodily movements with music, deepening and unifying three artistic experiments: music, movement, rhythm. The inventor of eurythmics, Emile Jacques Dalcroze, the author or *Rhythm, Music and Education*

(1922), exerted a profound influence on Claudel. The French dramatist went to Hellerau, where Dalcroze had founded his school, to study the techniques involved. Dalcroze believed that every gesture, facial nuance, rhythmic device must serve to exteriorise an inner voice. The actor must listen to this invisible world, see it, translate its message into plastic images, mobile moods, and spatial compositions. Claudel also believed in 'composing' a role, by gathering together the disparate parts of body and mind, and weaving them into a cohesive whole: internal and external movements must be made to work in harmony; accessories, like the synecdoche, must enhance the frame of reference; lighting must illuminate and order the spectacle; scenes must revolve around a specific *phare*, and thereby point up an inner architecture. Claudel's 'appetite for reality' compelled him to reject impressionism and opt for a synthetic approach to theatre.

'Break of Noon' (1905)

Break of Noon, which opened on 17 December, 1948, at the Marigny Theatre is a giant awakening in which the elements (sun, moon, earth, water) activate and energise the stage happenings. An animistic world is therefore brought to life, which allows the four characters on a ship sailing on the Indian ocean to China to bathe in primitive waters and to experience viscerally the mysterious and inexorable forces that are to decide their fate.[3]

The characters' names, interestingly, correspond to measurements. *Ysé* (wife, mother, and mistress; played by Edwige Feuillère) comes from the Greek *isos*, meaning 'equal', as are the two sides of an isosceles triangle. Iconographically, the *Y* in her name represents one form of the alchemical cross: unity which has become duality. No longer is Ysé the *one* woman who blends harmoniously into her surroundings, but rather one woman as opposed to the three men, her antagonists.

The name *De Ciz* (Ysé's husband; played by Jacques Dacqmine) signifies division, friction, and tension. Associated with the word *ciseaux* ('scissors'), *ciselure* ('carving'), and *ciseler* ('chiselling'), his name corresponds iconographically to his personality. He is weak, irresponsible, drawn here and there, cut off from himself and the world at large.

Mesa (the character who most closely resembles Claudel, who becomes Ysé's lover; played by Barrault) comes from the Greek *mesos*, meaning 'moderation' and 'balance'. But he is the antithesis of balance, and is given to extremes. Searching for beatitude, longing to give his life to God but prevented from doing so by his superiors, he has been thrust into a world of temptation, a den of iniquity.[4]

Amalric (played by Pierre Brasseur) is Ysé's second lover. His name may be divided into three syllables, corresponding to the three stages of life, the triangle, and the trinity. Strong, courageous, expansive, he is the very essence of masculinity – driven by a love of life, a need for conquest. He seeks to embrace a universe, encompass a world.

Act I begins with Amalric and Mesa on deck. The decors, designed by Félix Labisse, are stark in their simplicity: a ship and the necessary deck chairs, tables, portholes. The light is dazzling. A stillness permeates the atmosphere; a static nothingness, sameness. Mesa sums up the feeling: 'The days are so much alike they seem composed of a single great black and white day.' The sun pours down from an endless sky onto vast emptiness: water is everywhere. A kind of glorification of the void is implied here, a condition which enables beings to experience simplicity and detachment. The vessel navigating through the paradoxically burning/icy waters symbolises the human being in a spiritual quest, a soul in its mysterious wanderings. The protagonists understandably feel disoriented and dissatisfied. They exist in an aimless, goal-less sphere.

Unable to relate to others or give of himself, Mesa's solitary, taciturn nature needs recasting. Even Claudel described him as 'very hard, dry,' as 'antipathetical,' egotistical and preoccupied with himself and his own salvation: 'He has to be transformed', in any way possible.[5] Mesa's longing for God is his only preoccupation. It has become obsessive.

Ysé, blond, beautiful, sensual, and proud, needs to be loved and longs for the affection and security denied her by her husband. Only her senses have been aroused until now, not her soul. Her unfulfilled existence has made her consider herself 'a stranger' to the world at large, imprisoned in superficiality. Ysé is strong and elegant. Amalric describes her as a 'warrior,' a 'conqueror', and not a 'coquettish' person. She must 'subjugate' others, 'tyrannise', or else 'give herself' completely. Despite his implacable desire for Ysé, he quickly regains his composure, and he will not humble or weaken himself before her.

During the long days together, Ysé, the catalyst, will pave the way for Mesa's death and transfiguration. Why, he questions, has she been placed in his path? Why must she 'disturb' his 'peace of mind?' Serenity, not battle, is what his soul seeks; repose, not activity; indifference, not attachment. Mesa is aware that he will never be able to give himself completely to Ysé; that he can never be *one* during his life on earth: 'There is no way that I can give you my soul, Ysé.' There is, however, a side to Mesa which longs for earthly love despite all his statements concerning his spirituality: 'I long for love: O the joy of being fully loved!' When he is possessed by Ysé, his world begins to fall apart.

What was once a rigid attitude, a certainty, his desire to sacrifice his earthly existence to God, has become porous, weak, malleable.

Ysé poses a terrible conflict for Mesa. She has come between him and God. His feelings of guilt do not allow him to look her in the face. As their journey pursued its course, she forces their eyes to meet, pitilessly. Mesa looks away; refuses to share his pain with her; nor will he open his heart to her.

In Act II, the curtains open on a cemetery in Hong Kong, shaped like an omega. The sun has lost its glow; the heavens have darkened. The April monsoon season is about to erupt. An unformed, leaden, cloudy atmosphere envelops the scene. The blackness of the day and the omega-shaped cemetery are the perfect backdrop for the dismemberment and rebirth ritual to follow: the omega represents the final letter of the Greek alphabet and corresponds, therefore, to the beginning and end of a cycle of life. De Ciz, the 'watered down' husband, whose unstable nature will have to take on consistency if it is not to break up completely, decides to go on a dangerous mission into the heart of China. He stands to gain a lot of money. He leaves despite Ysé's pleas that he remain or at least take her with him.

Mesa, at the height of his power, radiating energy, meets Ysé in front of the cemetery. Neither looks at the other. Suddenly Ysé raises her head and opens her arms to him, and he embraces her, sobbing, crying out, 'It's all over.' The 'bridal chamber' is the cemetery. It is here that two archetypal figures are joined: that Mesa takes possession of Ysé. The sin has been committed. Time is abolished, the external world repudiated. Mesa and Ysé bathe in universal forces; their voices, like musical interludes, rhythmic sequences, acquire amplitude and depth. Onomatopoeias, metaphors, analogies, repetitions, alliterations take on the value of objects, which jar, bruise, abrade, and corrode as do chemicals biting their way through the elements; beauty is injured, patinas are destroyed, the whole is cut asunder.

In Act III the curtains open on a large room in a 'colonial' style house surrounded by verandas and enormous banyan trees in a port town in southern China. Mesa's inability to give himself wholeheartedly to Ysé led her to leave him a year prior to the events now taking place. Amalric is Ysé's lover and is caring for the child born to her and Mesa. Their happiness seems short-lived because of the insurrection taking place in China. Ysé and Amalric are to be killed, along with the other Europeans in the town. Rather than accept capture and possible torture, however, Amalric has set up a time bomb slated to blow up the entire building. They prefer to be masters of their destiny rather than passive recipients. Amalric faces his end as he has his life, with equanimity.

Ysé is more complex. Her thoughts focus on her past: her 'sins'. She lingers on her infidelities toward her husband, her abandonment of her children and her betrayal of Mesa. Death will serve a purpose, she feels. It will wash away her torment. She greets it not with fright, but with a kind of relief. Yet she feels trapped, anguished, and lines of grief mark her face.

Ysé hears a noise on the stairs. She shudders. The door opens. A shadow becomes visible; the form is reflected in a mirror in the room. Mesa enters. Ysé remains motionless and speechless. He questions her. Why hasn't she answered his letters? What has he done to deserve such treatment? He cannot live without her, he tells Ysé. Mesa grows irate because Ysé does not respond. He accuses her of having an 'iron' heart, a metallic personality, of being unbending, brittle. Ysé has branded him, fettered him. Mesa's anger mounts. He informs her of her husband's death, and the fact that they are now free to love each other 'without secret and without remorse'. He begs her to leave with him. He will save her from death and take her children with them. Mesa informs her that he has a pass for two people which will allow them through Chinese lines. Still Ysé remains silent. He approaches her; the dark flames of the sepulchral lamp he is carrying invade the scene, and their glow is reflected in Ysé's eyes and in the full-length mirror on the side of the stage. Mesa blows out the flame. Ysé has never really understood him, he declares vehemently.

Amalric enters. He strikes a match which lights up the room. The men look at each other. The action generated by the sulphur of the match symbolises the tension between Ysé's lovers: two sulphuric forces brought together. Mesa declares his intention of taking both mother and child with him. Amalric will give up neither. He asks Ysé to choose: to die with him or to live elsewhere with Mesa and the child. Mesa draws a weapon from his pocket. Amalric throws himself on him. Ysé watches the struggle in the mirror: an outer manifestation of an inner conflict.

The fight has ended. Amalric has thrown Mesa to the ground, where he lies broken in body and soul. His right shoulder has been dislocated; his leg 'demolished'. Amalric removes the 'pass' from Mesa's pocket. Ysé goes to the next room to get the infant. She remains there for a time and then returns alone. The child is dead. Amalric extinguishes the lamp. They leave. Ysé laughs hysterically.

In keeping with the classical monologue which French dramatists have been using since the seventeenth century to reveal a protagonist's inner conflict, Claudel wrote 'The Song of Mesa', also a monologue, but inspired by the Song of Songs. The biblical poetic dialogue between two lovers is considered by mystics to be an allegorical representation of

God, the bridegroom, and Israel, the bride; or the human soul in union with the divine beloved.

Moon rays now glow in the night atmosphere – as the theatre seems to have opened up on the entire universe. Stars and planets shine; their light corresponds to illumination fighting darkness in the soul; it is spirit in conflict with matter, fragmentation versus unity. The mystical noises made by the stars in what Barrault and Claudel both called this 'celestial kettle', teeming with energetic activity, with swarming sounds like the droning of bees, were composed by Honegger.[6]

Mesa's Song, uttered with poignancy and measure by Barrault, begins with a salute to the heavens above, the constellations, and the Queen of Heaven, that is the Virgin Mary, reminiscent of the image drawn of her in Revelation, standing on the crescent moon wearing a crown of stars. As Barrault sang out Mesa's incantation his diction utilised special rhythmic effects, intonations, and breathing patterns, in keeping with the pitches he sought to emphasise. He stressed accents and consonants, the length of certain syllables, allowing the musicality and vibrancy of the text to emerge. Nothing was left to inspiration; all was studied, like a musical score, beforehand. In Barrault's rendition, Mesa's voice became a protagonist, God speaking through man. His love for the terrestrial woman, Ysé, has now evolved from its existential impure condition to the dimensions of a cosmic figure: the matrix of the Christian world, a resplendent Moon Virgin. As moon rays flood the stage in a kind of epiphany, the dismal room is transformed into an awesome and majestic cathedral. Mesa's heart and mind – once exiled from Paradise by God, then geared to human needs, finally crushed and pulverised – have now been allowed to leave what he calls his 'detestable carcass'.[7]

Ysé returns; she walks through the room as if in a 'hypnotic trance.' The whiteness of her gown, the blondness of her hair, accentuated by the reflections of the moon rays in the mirror, concretise the sanctity of the preceding moments. Ysé goes to the room where the dead infant lies and cries strangely. Mesa calls to her. She returns and again passes in front of the 'spotless mirror' in search of something; then pauses, 'inundated by the moon', as Artemis, Isis, and the Virgin Mary had been when experiencing moments of similar sublimity.

Until now Ysé was a carnal female principle. As she walks toward Mesa and sits at his feet, however, he experiences her presence as a soul force, an anima. Their love has now been sublimated and bathed in pure visual essences. They are 'full of glory and light, creatures of God,' Ysé says. It was earthly love that had bound, tortured, and imprisoned her. No longer the sun-drenched Ysé on that August day at noon, she has become the Ysé of the night hours, of midnight. 'This is the Break of Noon,' she intones, 'And I am here, ready to be liberated.' The cycle has been completed. The number twelve, representing the New Jerusalem in Revelation, has become actualised for her (21:1). *Nox Profunda*. The great work has been completed. 'All veils have been dissipated and the Flesh now becomes Spirit.'

Although both protagonists are doomed to die, it is Ysé who emerges in her golden essence. Sacrifice, which leads to redemption, according to Claudel, does not seem to be authentic on Mesa's part. He returned to Ysé to take her and his child away with him. After his struggle with Amalraic he was physically unable to leave and the pass was taken from him; therefore the choice was no longer his, he could not escape. Ysé, on the other hand, of her own volition has chosen to return. Her sacrifice is profound and complete; it has earned her transfiguration and redeemed her from the weightiness of her earthly condition.

After the curtain came down on *Break of Noon*, Barrault 'had the strange and sublime impression he had produced a future classic.'[8] The critics agreed. They found his direction masterful and the entire spectacle momentous. Each of the actors was praised individually. Brasseur, as Amalric, was lauded for the passion, cruelty, and violence he put into his role of the cynical, lucid ravisher adventurer. Dacqmine, as De Ciz, exuding disquietude, for Feuillère's Ysé, she was the Eternal Feminine, a composite of gentleness and strength, plenitude and a lionesque quality, sensitivity and ruthlessness; sensual in all ways, she was the man-getter. Barrault played Mesa with intelligence and feeling, though many critics felt he did not have the physical stature to incarnate such a part. His face, however, was mobile and bore the disquieting and deeply rooted torment of a man at odds with the world and with himself.[9]

It is through the word that Claudel distills raw pain, humanises matter, descants brutalities, until subtle correspondences radiate in structured sequences, in blocks placed one upon the other, and en masse, assuming the power and stature of a cathedral, its foundations dug deep into the subsoil and its spires soaring toward divinity. Claudel's theatre is a complex of opposites: it contains the seed of both beauty and ugliness, happiness and despair, good and evil. The protagonists are all tainted with their opposites, bearing within their realms the spark of divine as well as Luciferian light and delight!

Conclusion

French theatre between the two World Wars reached a new high technically, philosophically, and psychologically. It saw a break with naturalism and impressionism; it witnesses an exploration into humankind's murky depths; it revealed a need to shear away the mask concealing those mephitic realms so deeply entrenched in individuals and societies.

Crommelynck and Ghelderode took a wry look at the world, creating sardonic and sadomasochistic visions of people and the society they had created. Theirs was savage comedy: humankind's motivations were despicable; individuals acted egotistically, ferociously, viciously. Sensitivity and tenderness were virtually banished from their world. When purity and beauty did emerge, infrequently, they were swept asunder by burgeoning evil. Satire and irony were the theatrical vehicles used by Crommelynck and Ghelderode to elicit powerful audience reaction. As their characters stalked the stage, each was cut open, their spiritual and psychological innards laid bare. To bruise, to hurt, to mock was the way of these playwrights, to arouse not mirth but rage, not belly laughter but malaise!

There were some optimists of sorts, and strangely enough, Tristan Tzara, the founder of Dadaism, was one of these. Why else would he have attempted to destroy conventions in all domains: literary, dramatic, political? Why else would he have wanted to wipe the slate clean if he didn't believe that someday society would be able to rectify its ways? Had he been a nihilist he would have remained passive and not sought to scandalise the world. Nor would he have called for a dismemberment of the status quo; or fostered an anti-logical and anti-rational approach to language and to the creative urge per se.

André Breton, the father of Surrealism, discovered the infinite riches embedded in the unconscious and was to reveal an unchartered realm; exciting, tenebrous, but also sublimely beautiful. By dislocating syntax, as had the Dadaists before them; by ridding theatre (and other art forms as well) of flesh-and-blood creatures, plots, and suspense; and by allowing the irrational to dominate, the Surrealists infused the performing arts with a new realism, anarchic to be sure, iconoclastic, aggressive, subversive, but different. Vitrac was one of the great innovators in this domain. Automaton-like and confused, his beings spoke the truth, cut through those hard crusts people and societies don to conceal what is considered unpalatable.

Artaud's 'theatre of cruelty' plumbed a metaphysical dimension. It sought to work on the spectators' nerves and senses, to whip up irrational contents – the true source of creativity. Drama existed everywhere. Plays, therefore, were to be performed in all sorts of areas: in temples, churches, and planetariums, and on the side of a mountain. Language was to take on the power of an incantation, as it had in ancient times. Lighting, sound effects, mime, gesture, every part of the spectacle, was to work together to create a cohesive whole, so as to arouse that primitive level within being. Theatre was a curative agent in the Aristotelian sense; it was not to be considered a pleasurable pastime.

Relatively classical in technique and vision, Cocteau, Giraudoux, Anouilh, and Claudel benefitted from the sensitive and creative direction of Pitoëff, Jouvet, Dullin, Barrault, and others. Choosing a mythical approach to theatre, they drew from a common heritage to bring forth the new, the provocative, and the evocative, enabling them to deal with problems both personal and collective. Cocteau's *Orpheus* underscored the antagonism existing between husband and wife, but it also emphasized the anguish of the poet who feels his creative instinct running dry. Giraudoux's *Ondine* and *The Madwoman of Chaillot* bring forth the differences existing between the pure in heart and the corrupt. Hope exists in Anouilh's *The Traveller Without Luggage*: individuals can, if they are firm and courageous, decide at least to a certain extent upon their destinies. Claudel's *Break of Noon* confronts audiences with questions of adultery, sacrifice, sadomasochism, and redemption in poignant poetic patterns rare in today's theatre.

Notes

Dates of reviews in newspapers are given in brackets as in note 5, chapter 3 (11.11.46).

PART I: DADA, SURREALISM AND THE THEATRE OF CRUELTY

1. André Breton, *Manifeste du Surréalisme*, p. 51.
2. Ibid., p. 11.
3. Louis Aragon, 'Une vague de rêves', *Commerce*, automne, 1924.
4. From Nadeau, *Surréalisme*, p. 45.

1. Tristan Tzara, 'The Gas Heart'

1. J. H. Matthews, *Theatre in Dada and Surrealism*, p. 18.
2. Michel Corvin, *Revue d'Histoire du Théâtre*, 1971–73. Le Théâtre existe-t-il?', p. 21.
3. Elmer Peterson, *Tristan Tzara*, p. 43.
4. Ibid., p. 35.
5. Micheline Tison-Braun, *Tristran Tzara inventeur de l'homme nouveau*, p. 7.
6. Corvin, p. 228.

7. Matthews, pp. 19–22.

8. Ibid., pp. 22–30.

9. Corvin, p. 255.

10. Ibid., p. 260.

11. Matthews, pp. 30–38. Quotes Henri Béhar, *Etude sur le Théâtre Dada et Surréaliste*, p. 159.

12. Ibid., p. 32.

13. Matthews, pp. 30–35.

14. Ibid., p. 20.

2. André Breton

1. André Breton, *Manifeste du Surréalisme*, p. 37.

2. Ibid., p. 34.

3. André Breton, *Les Pas perdus*, p. 9.

4. J. H. Matthews, *Theatre in Dada and Surrealism*, p. 88.

5. Ibid., p. 90.

6. Ibid., pp. 97–100.

3. Roger Vitrac, 'Victor'

1. Henri Béhar, *Roger Vitrac*, p. 18; 42–47.

2. Antonin Artaud, *Oeuvres complètes*, II, p. 14.

3. Ibid., II, p. 12.

4. Ibid., II, p. 267.

5. See J. H. Matthews, *Theatre in Dada and Surrealism*, pp. 109–32. From *Le Figaro littéraire* (11.11.46).

6. Roger Vitrac, *Théâtre*. Paris: Gallimard, 1946. All references to *Victor* comes from this edition. See Artaud, II, pp. 74–77.

7. Matthews, p. 129.

8. Béhar, pp. 185–190. The cast consisted of Juliette Greco, Mylène Gage, Christiane and Monique Lenier, Georges Malkine as the General, Yvan Pench, Claude Laurent, and Michel de Ré as Victor.

9. Ibid., p. 196. The cast included Claude Rich, Bernard Noël, Monique Mélinand, Uta Taeger, Hubert Deschamps, Odile Mallet, Nelly Benedetti, Alain Mottet. See Jean Anouilh, 'Roger Vitrac,' *Le Figaro* (1.10.62).

10. Artaud, II, p. 174.

Notes

4. Antonin Artaud, The Theatre of Cruelty

1. Antonin Artaud, *Oeuvres complètes*, I, pp. 74–81; p. 252.
2, Antonin Artaud, *The Theater and its Double*. Translated by Mary Caroline Richards, p. 71. See Bettina L. Knapp, *Antonin Artaud, Man of Vision*.
3. Ibid., pp. 65, 67.
4. Ibid., p. 116.
5. Ibid., pp. 85, 104.
6. Ibid., pp. 85, 134.
7. Ibid., pp. 135–6. See *Oeuvres complètes*, IV, 'Le Théâtre de Seraphin.'
8. *The Theater and its Double*, pp. 140, 110, 46.

PART II: FARCE, COMEDY, SATIRE

5. Fernand Crommelynck, 'The Magnificant Cuckold'

1. See Bettina L. Knapp, *Fernand Crommelynck*.
2. *The Magnificent Cuckold* opened on December 18, 1920 in Paris. Stella was played by R. Camier; the Nurse by Blanchini; Cornélie by Fernel; Leroy was Florence; Bruno was Lugné-Poë; Petrus was R. Weber; the Bourgemestre was Guy; the Cowherd was Noël; Estrugo was S. Plaute, the Count was Raoul.
3. Robert Kemp, *Le Monde* (1.22.46).
4. Guillot de Saix (9.10.21).
5. *Actors on Acting*. Edited by Toby Cole, p. 441.
6. Vsevolod Meyerhold, *Le Théâtre théâtral*, p. 171.
7. Meyerhold, pp. 155–57.
8. *L'Oeuvre* (18.9.41); *Paris-Midi* (6.9.41); *L'Atelier* (13.9.41).

6. Michel de Ghelderode, 'Escurial'

1. Michel de Ghelderode, 'Ostend Interviews,' in *Seven Plays*. Translated by George Hauger. I, p. 14.
2. André Vandegans, 'Les sources plastiques d'*Escurial*,' *Revue d'histoire du théâtre*, I, 1967, p. 26.
3. Michel de Ghelderode, *Théâtre*. I, p. 238.
4. André Alter, *L'Aube* (23.12.48); Catherine Valogne, *Arts* (24.12.48); Jean-Jacques Gautier, *Le Figaro* (27.12.48).

173

PART III: MYTHIC THEATRE

7. Jean Cocteau, 'Orpheus'

1. See Bettina L. Knapp, *Jean Cocteau*.
2. The cast was the following: Orpheus (Georges Pitoëff), Heurtebrise (Marcel Herrand), Eurydice (Ludmilla Pitoëff), Death (Mireille Havet), Azrael (Alfred Penay), Raphael (Georges de Vos). Sets were created by Jean-Victor Hugo; the costumes by Gabrielle Chanel.
3. André Beucler, *La Nouvelle Revue Française*, 17, 1926; *Chronique Dramatique d'études* (5.10.26); *Indépendent Belge* (17.10.26).

8. Jean Giraudoux, 'Ondine' and 'The Madwoman of Chaillot'

1. See Robert Cohen, *Giraudoux Three Faces of Destiny* and Bettina L. Knapp, *Louis Jouvet Man of the Theatre*.
2. The cast consisted of Le Chevalier Hans (Louis Jouvet), the Chambellan (Félix Oudart); Auguste (Romain Bouquet), the King of the Ondines (Auguste Bovério), Ondine (Madeleine Ozeray), Eugénie (Raymone), Bertha (Jeanne Hardeyn), Queen Iseult (Jeanne Reinhardt). The sets were created by Pavel Tchelitchew; the costumes, by Ira Belline; the music, by Henri Sauget.
3. Louis Jouvet, 'Dans les yeux de Giraudoux,' *Les Lettres françaises* (14.5.39).
4. Robert Kemp, *Le Temps* (5.5.39). *Feuilleton du Journal Le Temps* (8.5.39).
5. Emile Mass, *Le Petite bleu* (5.5.39); Robert Kemps, *Le Temps* (5.5.39); Benjamin Crémieux, *La Lumière* (12.5.39) *l'Age nouveau* (6.5.39); Lucien Descaves, *L'Intransigeant* (5.5.39).
6. André Warnold, 'J'ai épousseté le buste d'Electre,' *Le Figaro* (11.5.37).
7. The cast consisted of the Ragpicker (Louis Jouvet), the young man, Martial (Baconnet), the President (Félix Oudard), Irma (Monique Mélinand); Aurélia, the Madwoman of Chaillot

(Marguerite Moréno), Constance, the Madwoman of Passy (Marguerite Mayane); Gabrielle, the Madwoman of Saint-Sulpice (Raymone), Joséphine, the Madwoman of the Concorde (Lucienne Bogaert); some of the exploiters (Michel Etcheverry, Michel Grosse, Jean Bloch), etc. The sets and costumes were created by Christian Bérard.

8. Fabien Sollar, *Le Matin* (25.12.45); Pierre Lestinguez, *XX Siècle* (13.12.45); Jean-Jacques Gautier, *Le Figaro* (20.12.45); Maurice Schumann, *L'Aube* (21.12.45), Joseph Kessel, *France-Soir* (2.12.45).

9. Jean Giraudoux, *Le Théâtre complet*. VIII, p. 44.

9. Jean Anouilh, 'The Traveller Without Luggage'

1. Jean Anouilh, *Pièces brillantes*, p. 387.

2. See Alba della Fazia, *Jean Anouilh*; John Harvey, *Anouilh: A Study in Theatrics*; Leonard Pronko, *The World of Jean Anouilh*.

3. André Warnod, 'Interview avec Georges Pitoëff,' *Le Figaro* (16.2.37).

4. The cast consisted of Gaston (Georges Pitoëff); Madame Renaud (Marthe Mellot); Valentine (Nadine Picard); Georges Renaud (Louis Salou); the servants (Andrée Tainsy, Larive, Gaultier, Gobin), the little boy (Ludmilla Pitoëff); Duchess Dupont-Dufort (Nora Sylvère).

5. See Jean de Rigault, *Georges Pitoëff notre théâtre*.

6. Colette, *Journal* (22.2.37); Edmond Sée, *Oeuvre* (22.2.37); Madeleine Paz, *Populaire* (22.2.37); Lucien Dubech, *Candide* (4.3.37).

10. Paul Claudel, 'Break of Noon'

1. Paul Claudel, *Break of Noon*. Translated by Wallace Fowlie.

2. *Cahiers de Paul Claudel*, X, p. 198.

3. The cast consisted of Almaric (Pierre Brasseur), De Ciz (Jacques Dacqmine), Mesa (Jean-Louis Barrault), Ysé (Edwige Feuillère). The sets were created by Félix Labisse. The dresses worn by Ysé was designed by Christian Berard and executed by Piguet.

4. See Bettina L. Knapp, *Paul Claudel*.

5. Paul Claudel, *Mémoires improvisés*, p. 225.

6. *Cahiers Paul Claudel*, p. 210.

7. Ibid., p. 191.

8. Jean-Louis Barrault, *Reflexions sur le théâtre*, p. 201.

9. *Les Nouvelles littéraires*, 30, 12, 48; Raymond Cogniat, *Arts* (12.12.48); Jean-Jacques Gautier, *Le Figaro* (18.12.48); Justin Saget, *Combat* (5.3.48); Robert Kemp, *Le Monde* (19–20.12.48). See Jean-Louis Barrault, *Souvenirs pour demain*, pp. 206–215.

Bibliography

Actors on Acting, Edited by Toby Cole, edited by Toby Cole (New York: Crown, 1949).

Anouilh, Jean, *Pièces Roses* (Paris: La Table Ronde, 1958).

Anouilh, Jean, *Pièces Noires* (Paris: La Table Ronde, 1958).

Anouilh, Jean, 'Hommage à Jean Giraudoux,' *Chronique de Paris* (February 1951).

Anouilh, Jean, *Arts* (16.11.51).

Aragon, Louis, 'Une vague de rêves,' *Commerce* (Autumn 1924).

Artaud, Antonin, *Oeuvres complètes* (Paris: Gallimard, 1956–70).

Artaud Anthology, edited by Jack Hirschman (San Francisco: City Lights Books, 1965).

Antonin Artaud The Theatre and its Double, trans. by Mary Caroline Richards (New York: Grove Press, 1958).

Audiat, Pierre, *Paris Soir* (4.4.39).

Barrault, Jean-Louis, *Souvenirs pour demain* (Paris: Editions du Seuil, 1972).

Barrault, Jean-Louis, *Réflexions sur le théâtre* (Paris: Jacques Vautrain, 1949).

Jean-Louis Barrault Comme je le pense (Paris: Gallimard, 1975).

Baudelaire, Charles, *Oeuvres complètes* (Paris: Gallimard, 1961).

Béhar, Henri, *Roger Vitrac: Un Reprouvé du Surréalisme* (Paris: Nizet, 1966).

——————, Etude sur le théâtre Dada et Surréaliste (Paris: Gallimard, 1967).

Bergson, Henri, *Le Rire* (Paris: Presses universitaires de France, 1960).

Beyen, Roland, *Michel de Ghelderode* (Paris: Seghers, 1974).

Braun, Micheline-Tison, *Tristan Tzara Inventeur de l'Homme Nouveau* (Paris: Nizet, 1977).

Breton, André, Manifestes du Surréalisme (Paris: Gallimard, 1967).

—————— *Anthologie d'Humour Noir* (Paris: Jean Jacques Pauvert, 1966).

—————— and Philippe Soupault, 'Barrières,' *Les Champs magnétiques* [1920] suivi de *Vous m'oublierez et de s'il vous plait* (Paris: Gallimard, 1967).

—————— 'Lachez tout,' *Nouvelles littéraires* (1.4.22).

Cargill, Oscar, Fagin, Brullion, Fisher, William, *O'Neill and his Plays* (New York: New York University Press, 1963).

Cassou, Jean, *Le Monde* (22.11.66).

Castro, Nadine, *Le Théâtre de Michel de Ghelderode* (Lausanne: L'age d'Homme, 1979).

Claudel, Paul, *Partage de Midi* (Paris: Gallimard, 1949).

—————— *Break of Noon*, trans. Wallace Fowlie (Chicago: H. Regnery Co. 1960).

—————— Mémoires improvisés (Paris: Gallimard, 1969).

Cahiers Paul Claudel, X (Paris: Gallimard, 1974).

Cocteau, Jean, *Oeuvres complètes* (Genève: 1946–1951).

Cohen, Robert, *Giraudoux Three Faces of Destiny* (Chicago: University of Chicago Press, 1958).

Corvin, Michel, 'Le Théâtre Dada existe-t-il?' *Revue d'histoire du théâtre* (1971–73).

Crommelynck, Fernand, *Oeuvres complètes* (Paris: Gallimard, 1967).

Encyclopedie du Théâtre contemporain, II (Paris: Olivier Perrin, 1959).

Fazia, Alba della, *Jean Anouilh* (New York: Twayne Publishing Co., 1969).

Bibliography

Feiblemen, James, *In Praise of Comedy* (New York: Russell and Russell, 1962).

Frank, André, *Georges Pitoëff* (Paris: L'Arche, 1958).

Freud, Sigmund, *The Basic Writings* (New York: Random House, 1939).

Ghelderode, Michel de, *Théâtre* (Paris: Gallimard, 1950–57).

—————— 'Ostend Interviews,' *Seven Plays*, trans. George Hauger (New York: Hill and Wang, 1969).

Gignoux, Hubert, *Jean Anouilh* (Paris: Editions du Temps Présent, 1946).

Giraudoux, Jean, *Oeuvres complètes* (Neuchâtel: Ides et Calendes 1945–51).

Grossvogel, David, *The Self-Conscious Stage in Modern French Drama* (New York: Columbia University Press, 1958).

Guicharnaud, Jacques, *Modern French Theatre from Giraudoux to Beckett* (New Haven: Yale University Press, 1961).

Harding, Esther, *Psychic Energy* (Princeton: Princeton University Press, 1973).

Harvey, John, *Anouilh: A Study in Theatrics* (New Haven: Yale University Press, 1964).

Ionesco, Eugène, *Notes et Contre-Notes* (Paris: Gallimard, 1966).

Jouvet, Louis, 'Dans les yeux de Giraudoux,' *Les Lettres françaises* (14.5.45).

Kemp, Robert, *Le Monde* (22.1.46).

Kirstein, Lincoln, *Dance* (New York: Dance Horizon Republications, 1969).

Knapp, Bettina, *Louis Jouvet Man of the Theatre* (New York: Columbia University Press, 1958).

—————— *Jean Cocteau* (New York: Twayne Publishers, 1970).

—————— *Fernand Crommelynck* (Boston: Twayne Publishers, 1978).

—————— *Paul Claudel* (New York: Frederick Ungar, 1982).

—————— *Antonin Artaud Man of Vision* (Athens: Ohio University Press, 1980).

Knowles, Dorothy, *French Drama of the Inter-War Years* (New York: Barnes and Noble, 1968).

Lenormand, H.-R., *Les Pitoëff* (Paris: Odette Lieutier, 1943).

L'Oeuvre (18 septembre, 1941).

Lorand, Sandor, *Perversions* (New York: Grammercy Books, 1956).

Luppe, Robert de, *Anouilh* (Paris: Classiques du XX siècle, 1959).

Magny, Claude-Edmonde, *Précieux Giraudoux* (Paris: Editions du Seuil, 1945).

Marsh, Edwin Owen, *Jean Anouilh: Poet of Pierrot and Pantalon* (London: W. H. Allen, 1953).

Matthews, J. H., *Theatre in Dada and Surrealism* (Syracuse: Syracuse University Press, 1974).

Meyerhold, Vsevolod, *Le Théâtre théâtral*, translated by Nina Gourfinkel (Paris: Gallimard, 1963).

Nadeau, Maurice, *Histoire du surréalisme* (Paris: Editions du Seuil, 1964).

Oxenhandler, Neal, *Scandal and Parade: The Theatre of Jean Cocteau* (New Brunswick: Rutgers University Press, 1957).

Paris Midi (9.5.41).

Peterson, Elmer, *Tristan Tzara* (New Brunswick: Rutgers University Press, 1971).

Pronko, Leonard, C, *The World of Jean Anouilh* (Berkeley: University of California Press, 1961).

Sypher, Wylie, *Comedy* (New York: A Doubleday Anchor Book, 1956).

Vandegans, André, 'Les sources plastiques d'Escurial,' *Revue d'Histoire du théâtre* (1967).

Vitrac, Roger, *Théâtre* (Paris: Gallimard, 1964).

Warnold, André, 'J'ai epousseté le buste d'Electre,' *Le Figaro Litteraire* (11.5.37).

———— 'Interview avec Georges Pitoëff,' *Le Figaro* (16.2.37).

Appendix

TRISTAN TZARA:

La première Aventure céleste de Monsieur Antipyrine, created on 27 March, 1920, at the Dada demonstration in Paris. Set and costumes designed by Francis Picabia.

La deuxième Aventure céleste de Monsieur Antipyrine, created on 26 May, 1920 at the Galerie Montaigne.

Le Coeur à gaz, created on 10 June, 1921 at the Galerie Montaigne.

Mouchoir de Nuages, created 17 May, 1904 at the Théâtre de la Cigalle.

ANDRÉ BRETON AND PHILIPPE SOUPAULT:

S'il vous plaît was created on 27 March, 1920 at the Salle Berlioz.

Vous m'oublierez, created in 1920 at the Salle Gaveau.

ROGER VITRAC

Le Peintre, published in January 1922.

Entrée libre, dated 28 November, 1922.

Les mystères de l'amour, created on 2 June, 1927 by the Théâtre Alfred Jarry. Directed by Antonin Artaud.

Victor ou les Enfants au pouvoir, created on 24 December, 1928 by the Théâtre Alfred Jarry. directed by Antonin Artaud.

Appendix

Le Coup de Trafalgar, created on 8 June, 1934 at the Théâtre de l'Atelier.
Le Camelot, created on 12 October, 1936 at the Théâtre de l'Atelier.
Directed by Charles Dullin; music by Georges Auric; sets by
Touchagues and costumes by Mme Schiaparelli.

ANTONIN ARTAUD:

Le Jet de Sang, 1927.
The Cenci, created on 6 May, 1935 at the Folies-Wagram.

FERNAND CROMMELYNCK:

Le Sculpteur de masques, created on 1 February, 1911 at the Théâtre du
Ggymnase.
Nous n'irons plus au bois, created on 28 April, 1906 at the Théâtre du
Parc, Brussels.
Le Marchand de regrets, created in 1913 at the Théâtre du Parc in
Brussels.
Le Cocu magnifique, created on 20 December, 1920 at the Théâtre de
l'Oeuvre in Paris. Directed by Lugné-Poë. The Moscow production in
1922 was directed by Vsevolod Meyerhold; sets by L. P. Popova.
Les Amants puérils, created on 14 March, 1921 at the Comédie
Montaigne in Paris. Directed by Gaston Baty.
Tripes d'Or, created on 29 April, 1925 at the Comédie des Champs-
Elysées. Directed by Louis Jouvet.
Carine or *Ou la jeune fille folle de son âme*, created on 29 December, 1929
at the Théâtre de l'Oeuvre. Directed by Lugné-Poë.
Une Femme qu'a le coeur trop petit, created on 11 January, 1934 at the
Comédie des Champs-Elysées. Directed by Pauline Pax.
Chaud et Froid or *L'idee de Monsieur Dom*, created on 24 November,
1934 at the Comédie des Champs-Elysées.

MICHEL DE GHELDERODE (first performances in France)

La Mort du Docteur Faust, created on 27 January, 1928 at the Groupe Art
et Action.
Christophe Colomb, created on 25 October, 1929 at the Groupe Art et
Action.
Escurial, created on 17 January, 1949 at the Studio des Champs Elysées.
Directed by Rene Dupuy and Michel Vitold.
Mademoiselle Jaïre, created in June, 1949, at the Théâtre des Noctam-
bules. Directed by André Reybaz.

Appendix

Hop Signor! created on 22 November, 1949 at the Théâtre des Noctambules. Directed by André Reybaz.

Sire Halewyn, created on 17 February, 1950 at the Théâtre des Noctambules. Directed by Catherine Toth.

Barabbas, created on 21 February, 1950 at the Théâtre de l'Oeuvre.

Ballade du Grand Macabre, 1953 at the Studio des Champs-Elysées. Directed by René Dupuy; sets by Jacques Marillier.

L'Ecole des bouffons, created in 1953 at the Théâtre de l'Oeuvre. Directed by Marcel Lupovici; sets by Raymond Raynal.

Magie Rouge, created in April 1956 at the Théâtre du Quartier Latin. Directed by Gilles Chancrin.

Trois Acteurs, un drame, created in July 1958 at the Théâtre de Poche. Directed by Gilles Chancrin.

Les Aveugles, created in 1958 at the Théâtre de Poche. Directed by Gilles Chancrin.

JEAN COCTEAU

Parade, created in Rome in 1916 at the Théâtre du Chatelet in Paris in 1917. Choreographed by Léonide Massine; music by Erik Satie; sets and costumes by Picasso.

Les Mariés de la Tour Eiffel, created on 18 June, 1921 at the Théâtre des Champs-Elysées. Choreography by Jean Cocteau; sets by Irène Lagut; costumes and masks by Jean Hugo; music by Les Six.

Antigone (adaptation of Sophocles), created on 20 December, 1922 at the Théâtre de l'Atelier. Directed by Charles Dullin; sets by Picasso.

Roméo et Juliette (adaptation of Shakespeare), created in June at the Théâtre de la Cigale. Directed by Jean Cocteau; sets by Jean Hugo.

Orphée, created on 17 June, 1926 at the Théâtre des Arts. Directed by Georges Pitoeff; sets by Jean Hugo.

La Voix humaine, created on 17 February, 1930 at the Comédie-Française. Sets by Christian Bérard.

La Machine infernale, created on 10 April, 1934 at the Comédie des Champs-Elysées. Directed by Louis Jouvet; sets by Christian Bérard.

Oedipe-Roi (adaptation of Sophocles), created in June, 1937 at the Théâtre Antoine. Directed by Jean Cocteau; sets by G. Monin.

Les chevaliers de la Table Ronde, created on 14 October, 1937 at the Théâtre de l'Oeuvre. Directed by Jean Cocteau; sets by Jean Cocteau.

Les Parents terribles, created on 14 November, 1938 at the Théâtre des Ambassadeurs. Directed by Alice Cocea; sets by G. Monin.

Les Monstres sacrés, created on 17 February, 1940 at the Théâtre Michel. Directed by Andre Brule; sets by Christian Bérard.

L'Aigle a deux tetes, created in November, 1946 at the Théâtre Hebertot; sets by André Beaurepaire.

Bacchus, created 20 November, 1951 at the Théâtre Marigny. Directed by Jean Cocteau; sets by Jean Cocteau.

Appendix

JEAN GIRAUDOUX

Siegfried, created on 3 May, 1928 at the Comédie des Champs-Elysées. Directed by Louis Jouvet; sets by Camille Cipra.

Amphitryon, created on 8 November, 1929 at the Comédie des Champs-Elysées. Directed by Louis Jouvet; sets by Camille Cipra.

Judith, created on 5 November, 1932 at the Théâtre Pigalle. Directed by Louis Jouvet; sets by Jouvet and René Moulaert.

Intermezzo, created on 27 February, 1933 at the Comédie des Champs-Elysées. Directed by Louis Jouvet; sets by L. Leyritz.

Tessa (adaptation of M. Kennedy), created on 14 November, 1934 at the Théâtre de l'Athénée. Directed by Louis Jouvet; sets by René Moulaert.

La Guerre de Troie n'aura pas lieu, created on 21 November, 1935 at the Théâtre de l'Athénée. Directed by Louis Jouvet; sets by Mariano Andreu.

Supplement au Voyage de Cook, created on 21 November, 1935 at the Théâtre de l'Athénée. Directed by Louis Jouvet; sets by Mariano Andreu.

Electre, created on 13 May, 1937 at the Théâtre de l'Athénée. Directed by Louis Jouvet; sets by G. Monin.

L'Impromptu de Paris, created on 4 December, 1937 at the Théâtre de l'Athénée. Directed by Louis Jouvet; sets by Vuillard.

Cantique des cantique, created on 12 October, 1938 at the Comédie Française. Directed by Louis Jouvet; sets by G. Monin.

Ondine, created on 3 May, 1939 at the Théâtre de l'Athénée. Directed by Louis Jouvet; sets by Pavel Tchelitchew.

L'Apollon de Marsac, created on 16 June, 1942 in Rio de Janeiro. Directed by Louis Jouvet; sets by E. Anahory.

La Folle de Chaillot, created on 22 December, 1945 at the Théâtre de l'Athénée. Directed by Louis Jouvet; sets by Christian Bérard.

Pour Lucrèce, created on 4 November, 1953 at the Théâtre Marigny. Directed by Jean-Louis Barrault; sets by A. M. Cassandre.

JEAN ANOUILH:

L'Hermine, created on 26 April, 1932 at the Théâtre de l'Oeuvre. Mise-en-scène by Paulette Pax.

Le Voyageur sans bagage, created on 16 February, 1937 at the Théâtre des Mathurins. Directed by Georges Pitoëff, sets by Georges Pitoëff.

Le Bal des voleurs, created on 17 September, 1938 at the Théâtre des Arts. Directed by André Barsacq who also did the sets and costumes. Music by Darius Milhaud.

La Sauvage, created on 10 January, 1938 at the Théâtre des Mathurins. Directed and sets by Georges Pitoëff. Music by Darius Milhaud.

Appendix

Léocadia, created in November, 1940 at the Théâtre de la Michodière. Directed by Pierre Fresnay. Music of Francis Poulenc.

Antigone, created on 4 February, 1944 at the Théâtre de l'Atelier. Directed and sets by André Barsacq.

L'Invitation au château, created on 5 November, 1947 at the Théâtre de l'Atelier. Directed and sets by André Barsacq. Music by Francis Poulenc.

La Valse des toréadors, created on 9 January, 1952 at the Comédie des Champs-Elysées. Directed and sets by J.-D. Maclès.

L'Alouette, created on 14 October, 1953 at the Théâtre Montparnasse-Gaston Baty. Sets by J.-D. Maclès.

Medee, created on 25 March, 1953 at the Théâtre de l'Atelier. Sets and costumes by Andre Bakst. Directed by Andre Barsacq. *Ornifle ou le courant d'air*, created on 7 November, 1955 at the Comédie des Champs-Élysées. Directed by Roland Piétri.

L'Hurluberlu ou le réactionnaire amoureux, created on 5 February, 1959 at the Comédie des Champs-Elysées. Directed by Roland Piétri.

Becket or *L'Honneur de Dieu*, created on 1 October, 1959 at the Théâtre Montparnasse-Gaston Baty. Sets and costumes by J.-D. Maclès; directed by Jean Anouilh and Roland Piétri.

PAUL CLAUDEL

L'Annonce faite à Marie, created on 22 December, 1912 at the Théâtre de l'Oeuvre. Directed by Lugne-Poe; sets by Jean Variot.

L'Echange, created on 22 January, 1914 at the Théâtre du Vieux-Colombier. Directed by Jacques Copeau; sets by Doucet.

L'Otage, created on 5 June, 1914 at the Théâtre de l'Oeuvre. Directed by Lugné-Poë; sets by Jean Variot.

Partage de Midi, created on 12 November, 1916 by the Groupe Art et Action. Sets by Autant-Lara, Autant and Giraud; 16 December, 1948 at the Théâtre Marigny. Directed by Jean-Louis Barrault; sets by Félix Labisse.

Tête d'Or, created on 25 April, 1924 at the Groupe Art et Action. Directed by Mme. Lara; sets by Georges Valmier.

Le Pain dur, created in October, 1926 at the Landestheater, Oldenburg. Directed by Hans Pretz.

La Père humilié, created on 26 November, 1928 at the Schauspielhaus, Dresden. Directed by Joseph Gielen; sets by Malinke.

Le Repos du septième jour, created on 10 December, 1928 at the Narodowy Theatre, Warsaw. Directed by Radulski; sets by Drabik.

Le Livre de Christophe Colomb, created on 5 May, 1930 at the Staatsoper unter den Linden, Berlin. Directed by M. Horts; sets by M. Araventinos. Music by Darius Milhaud.

Appendix

La Ville, created in February 1931 at the Salle Patria, Brussels. Directed by A. van de Velde.

Protee, created on 4 April, 1933 at the Municipal Theatre, Amsterdam. Students' Dramatic Association.

Les Choéphores (translation of Aeschylus) created on 27 March, 1935. Brussels.

Jeanne au bucher, created on 6 May, 1939 at the Theatre Municipal d'Orleans. Music by A. Honegger; sets by Alexandre Benois.

Le Soulier de satin, created on 27 November, 1943 at the Comédie-Française. Directed by Jean-Louis Barrault; sets by Lucien Couteaud.

La Jeune fille Violaine, created in March, 1944 at the Salle Iena. Directed by Maurice Leroy; sets by Maurice Leroy.

L'Histoire de Tobie et de Sara, created on 5 September, 1947 at Avignon. Directed by Maurice Cazeneuve.

Index

187

Index

Index

190

Index

Index